HEALING MINISTRY

Experiences with Viktor E. Frankl's Logotherapy in *Psychiatry*, *Psychology*, *Clinical Counselling*, and *Psychotherapy*

(Selected Articles from the Authors' Clinical Practice)

HEALING MINISTRY

Experiences with Viktor E. Frankl's Logotherapy in
Psychiatry, *Psychology*, *Clinical Counselling*, and
Psychotherapy

(Selected Articles from the Authors' Clinical Practice)

MARIA MARSHALL, Ph.D.

and

EDWARD MARSHALL, Ph.D.

Ottawa, Ontario

Canada
2013

ISBN-10: 1482668874; ISBN-13: 978-1482668872

Ottawa Institute of Logotherapy
PO Box 45006
Ottawa, ON K2M 2G0
Canada

www.logotherapy.ca

Dedicated to Peter Marshall (With love: Your Parents) E.M. & M.M.

HEALING MINISTRY

TABLE OF CONTENTS

Introduction

Healing Ministry is based on our experiences of using Viktor E. Frankl's Logotherapy during the past twenty years. It is based upon selected articles we wrote on our experience working as Psychiatrist (Dr. Edward Marshall), Psychologist (Dr. Maria Marshall), Clinical Counsellor and Psychotherapist (Drs. Maria and Edward Marshall).

The first article *"Healing Through Meaning"* was written by Maria Marshall in 1994. It was submitted in preparation for the Tenth World Congress on Logotherapy, which was held in July, 1995. The paper was presented in an abbreviated format. This was the first *International Conference on Logotherapy* that Maria attended. At that time, she was fresh from completing her Bachelor's Degree in Psychology with Honours, at the University of Calgary, in Alberta, (where she conducted an Observational Study of Parent-Child Dyadic Interactions, appearing in a later Chapter, as part of her Honours Thesis).

In 1994, she formally started her studies in the Counselling and Human Development Program of Hardin-Simmons University, in Abilene, Texas. She had the opportunity to study with Dr. Robert C. Barnes, Chair of the Department, as well as the President of the International Board of Directors of the Viktor Frankl Institute. The Tenth World Congress allowed her to meet and to study with other distinguished Logotherapists, such as Dr. Elisabeth Lukas.

The second article, *"Seeds of Reconciliation in Logotherapy,"* was written in 2000. It was submitted for presentation at an International Conference on Logotherapy, which was scheduled for the year 2001, in Rome, Italy. Unfortunately, in the wake of the terrorist attacks in September 11, 2001, the conference was cancelled. The paper has been recently re-constructed with help from Dr. Edward Marshall, and appears in this text. A shorter version of it has been submitted as an article for publication in the *International Forum for Logotherapy* (IFL).

The third article *"Logotherapeutic Principles in Marriage Therapy"* was written in the same year, 2000, and was presented at the International Conference of Transcultural Psychiatry in

Andorra, in 2001. The photo on our cover page was taken in Andorra. It is entitled "The Dancing Couple" and is the most photographed statue and symbol of the Principality of Andorra.

The trip to Andorra was Dr. Maria Marshall's first exposure to Spanish language and culture. Her memories of this friendly, small Principality are still very vivid.

Shortly after the conference in Andorra, Dr. Maria Marshall and Dr. Edward Marshall met. Dr. Edward Marshall, at the time was working in the United Kingdom as Psychiatrist. While Maria is originally from the north part of the Hungarian speaking region of Voivodina, of the former Yugoslavia, Edward is originally from the Canary Islands. Although the two of us originally come from distant countries from each other in Europe, we felt a connection beyond the limits of state boundaries.

"*Families and the Search for Meaning*" is a recent writing (2012), and it is based on our past ten years of marriage and family life together. Raising our children is helping us to appreciate the challenges of balancing work life and home life, and creating a safe and nurturing environment for our children, where they feel protected, and valued. Our aim is to aid other families who encounter similar challenges.

The fifth article "*The Role of Logotherapy-Education in the Treatment of Personality Disorders*" is based on Dr. Edward Marshall's work as Psychiatrist, and Psychotherapist. During his many years of experience of treating people with Personality Disorders, Dr. Marshall came to appreciate and to integrate the principles of Viktor Frankl's Logotherapy into his everyday practice. It was recently submitted for presentation at the upcoming Fourteenth World Congress on Logotherapy, in Dallas, Texas, in June, 2013.

The sixth article "*Logotherapy and the Physical Health of People Suffering with Mentally Ill Patients*" was written by Dr. Edward Marshall in 1995, on the occasion of Dr. Viktor E. Frankl's one hundredth birthday anniversary. It is based on his experiences of working as Family Physician (in Spain), and Psychiatrist in the United Kingdom.

The seventh, and last article, *"From Emotional Suffering to Triumph: Building Courage Through 'The Rainbow Exercise,'"* is a recent article by Dr. Maria Marshall (2013), submitted for publication in the IFL. Its purpose is to inspire courage and hope for clients and therapists, and draws on her self-experience of parent, and therapist.

Throughout our past twenty years of practice, we came in contact with hundreds and thousands of individuals, from all walks of life, presenting various emotional, psychological, and spiritual challenges in their lives. We are grateful to them for their trust and confidence in us. We are also hopeful, that the wellspring of our experience in these selected articles can be a useful resource to therapists and to clients who are called to participate in the *Healing Ministry*.

Chapter I

Healing Through Meaning

Our world is a world of paradoxes: Day-by-day, we hear of spreading violence, and of the heroism of those trying to fight it; we hear of devastating wars destroying the unity of once strong and prosperous countries, and witness reconciliation among age-old enemies.

Day-by-day, we are shattered by the pain experienced by our loved ones and receive encouragement from those who, despite all the suffering they have experienced in their past, lift their eyes to the stars of heaven and march forward with a prayer on their lips knowing that there is hope in times of despair, there is light in the darkness of the night, there is courage to be found in fighting weakness, and power in confronting death.

In our times, we realize, that changes are imminent--we sense the need to reach out if we want to remain human--yet, we often feel that the meaning of a particular situation, the meaning of this or that moment is already determined by our current needs, emotions, and wants.

Frequently, the urge to dominate, to "be in control," to achieve our goals, or to fulfill our dreams, appears to block our receptivity to the voice of the ultimate, the never-ceasing, and never-ending. In our quest for power, we want to be in control here-and-now, we want to be free here-and-now; we want to experience pleasure here-and-now.

In many situations, we are not concerned about others. Rather, we want to know "*What is in it for us?*", or "*What is in it for me?*" (Barnes, 1993). We ask, "*What can I, personally, get out of this event?,*" instead of "*What can I give to others?*". "*How can I make the world a better place to live in?*"--"*What is my unique contribution to the welfare of the world?*" seems to be the predominant dilemma facing us today.

In our increasingly mechanized world, there seems to be less and less place for questions like "*What is my unique task in the order of creation?*", "*Where is my area of freedom?*", "*Where am I, as a person, an unrepeatable and irreplaceable unity?*"

This then, results in a threefold distortion of in our eyes: (1) it gives us a false concept of freedom to aim at, (2) it encourages us to "wash our hands,", to try to free ourselves from the responsibility for our actions, and to "passively swim with the tide," (3) and such an attitude prevents us from living a fully human life, causing us to feel that our existence and struggles are meaningless and absurd (Ungar, 1993).

Sooner or later, however, we come to the realization that the struggle for power, pleasure, and success can never directly lead to the true reward--inner happiness and satisfaction (Barnes, 1993). On the contrary, it results in endless frustrations, feelings of anxiety, because we come to think that "It seems to make no difference of what we do, life is uncontrollable." At this point our despair turns into a sense of helplessness and hopelessness followed by apathy and depression. These are the manifestations of living in an "existential vacuum" (Frankl, 1967; p.31), which is perhaps one of the most common ailments of our society.

The term existential vacuum is best described as the feeling of inner emptiness and inner void, of lacking values, purpose, and meaning in life, or, as being in a state of "weightlessness," that is, existing without any forces to be pushed or pulled by (Barnes, 1994).

Having found no meaning in life facilitates one to mobilize his or her powers toward the direction of filling this emptiness with other, supposedly compensating activities, promising short-term pleasure or satisfaction. These can include things such as violence, sex, drugs, defiance of authority, and many types of neurotic behavior (Lukas, 1986b). These misguided attempts at securing one's "little heaven" here on earth are, on the other hand, constantly plagued by deflation, diminishment, and even more intense craving. Finally, the person is left with the uneasy feeling of un-fulfillment, frustration, abandonment, anger, and disgust. All these symptoms are exacerbated by further effort to try to conceal or deny the debilitating reality of having lost one's power to be in control.

Other times, misfortunes and tragedies happen that shatter even those "strong in their faith." Accidents, incurable disease, or natural disasters may strike our families, claim the life of innocent victims, or cause irreparable damage. Life seems to stop for a while for the victims, as they try to cope with their intense feelings of anger and guilt, questioning what meaning is left in life?

Those who have experienced the "darkness of the depths" will verify that there is probably nothing more painful for us, and nothing more anxiety provoking, than the realization of a lost sense of belongingness and wholeness--the suffering that results from a loss of meaning and purpose in life (Ungar, 1994). Those who have known heartbreak in life, those who have experienced pain, guilt, and death (the tragic triad of human existence: Frankl, 1975, p. 125), will confirm that there is nothing more annihilating, despairing, and destroying for us, than the thought that this suffering is meaningless. It does not serve any purpose and does not lead to any good (Frankl, 1975). Indeed, hopelessness, following the realization of the futility of one's life is the best predictor of one's potential to commit suicide (Barnes, 1994).

However, there can be something "enlightening" about this pain that we experience in times of great despair. Namely, it can lead us to questioning our lifestyle that resulted in unhappiness and the values we blindly followed up to the point of finding ourselves in the "valley" upon a fast descent from the "top." Suffering may reawaken our thirst for the ultimate-- the search for meaning (Frankl, 1975). It may open our eyes to see that true happiness is the result of a fully lived life, rather than of a life filled with happiness (Fabry, 1994).

From the perspective of logotherapy, existence means a certain kind of being (Frankl, 1967). An essential characteristic of human existence is self-transcendence (Frankl, 1965). Through self-transcendence, we can transcend our environment, and more than that, we can transcend our being toward that which is intended. That which alone is meaningful gives our life a new direction to move into. It gives a goal to strive toward, and a destination to reach.

When we transcend our circumstances, we rise above the realm of our somatic and psychic dimensions, and enter the realm of the genuinely human. We enter a new dimension--the "noetic dimension"--which is the dimension of the spirit (Frankl, 1985; p. 23). The ability to reach beyond ourselves is the key to the treasure trove of our existence. It is the key to our will to say "yes" to life, despite everything. It is the key to our becoming more of what we were created to be.

One of the basic tenets of logotherapy is that we are three dimensional beings. We have a somatic dimension (constituted by our bodies), we have a psychic dimension (constituted by our mind), and, in addition to these two dimensions--which are also found in animals--we have a third dimension--unique to us humans--the noetic dimension (the dimension of the spirit (Fabry, 1994; p. 17). The spiritual dimension, together with the physical and psychic dimensions, makes us unique, unrepeatable, and irreplaceable entities.

"The three dimensions of human existence should not be thought of as layers existing on the top of each other, rather, the physical, psychic, and spiritual dimensions exist as interacting components of one unique and complete entity--the human person" (Fabry, J., 1994; p. 20).

Our somatic dimension (or body) is largely restricted to the things we "*must*" do. It is the dimension affected and shaped by genetic and environmental influences, as well as the seat of instinctual drives seeking satisfaction. All processes in the realm of the soma (the body) move in the direction of satisfaction, followed by a resting state--homeostasis (Frankl, 1985; p. 63).

Our psychic dimension (mind) is concerned with what we "*can*" do. Although the development of the mind is influenced by genetic and environmental effects, its capacity, at all times, reaches beyond the essential nature of its components (the collection of nerve cells). The mind is capable of conscious thought, rational thinking, planning, and problem solving. The mind is the seat of our subjective experiences of form, color and quality, as well as the source of most of our desires and needs seeking fulfillment.

Unlike drives arising from the somatic dimension, however, the motivating forces of the psychic dimension can never be fully satisfied. At best, we can achieve a reasonable balance between them.

While the somatic and psychological aspects of our being are more or less hereditary, and, thereby limiting, together with our noetic (spiritual) dimension, they form a whole, which is not restricted solely to what we "must" or "can" do, but rather, our whole being is oriented toward what we "*ought*" to do.

The spiritual dimension is characterized by a continuous tension between what one "must" do, what one "can" do, and what-one "ought" to do. This healthy tension is what logophilosophy terms as *Noo-dynamics* (Frankl, 1967; p. 59). We continuously experience a healthy tension between those numerous options we have. Our task is to choose the one our conscience, functioning as an "*inner compass*," (Barnes, 1994; p. 15) points in the direction of; the one that would be the most fulfilling, and the most meaningful.

Through the choices we make, all of us are called to develop our unique potentials, and to grow closer to that eternal source of love, of whose mercy we exist. We are called to choose the option most pleasing to God.

"Viktor Frankl once said that God is not something that exists in the human dimension. He exists in a different dimension altogether; he is the ground of existence. Maybe, he is the coordinate system itself" (Fabry, 1994; p. 165).

Through the dimension of the spirit, we are ultimately connected to this coordinate system. Our existence is interwoven with the existence of the coordinate system itself-- with the existence of God. The highest meaning in this coordinate system is, therefore, determined by the coordinate system itself.

Life lived from the point of view of transcendence is a gift of God, which transcends human nature itself, inexplicably uniting God and human. As Jesus reminded Nicodemus, "*A person is born physically of human parents, but he is born spiritually of the Spirit*" (John 3:5).

Perhaps no words express our relationship with God more beautifully than those of Carl Jung who wrote:

"Whatever one can say, no words can express the whole. To speak of partial aspects is always too much or too little, for only the whole is meaningful. 'Love bears all things and endures all things' (1 Cor. 13:7). These words say all there is to be said; nothing can be abandoned to them. For we are in the deepest sense the victims and the instruments of cosmological 'LOVE.' I put the word in quotation marks to indicate that I do not use it in its connotations of desiring, preferring, favoring, wishing, and similar feelings, but as something superior to the individual, a unified and undivided whole. Being part, man cannot grasp the whole. He is at its mercy. He may assent to it, rebel against it; but he is always caught up by it and enclosed within it. He is dependent upon it and sustained by it. Love is his light and darkness, whose end he cannot see. 'Love ceases not'--whether he speaks with the 'tongues of angels' or with scientific exactitude traces the cell down to its uttermost source. Man can try to name LOVE, showering upon it all the names at his command, and still he

will involve himself in endless self-deceptions. If he possesses a grain of wisdom, he will lay down his arms and call the unknown by the name of unknown, IGNOTUM PER IGNOTIUS--that is by the name of God. That is a confession to his subjection, his imperfection, and his dependence; but at the same time it is a testimony to choose between truth and error" (Jung, 1964; p. 275).

Our relationship with God is a continuous giving and receiving (Ungar, 1994; p. 22). We respond to God's call through our actions, which reflect our attitudes and values. In return, we receive love, joy, patience, kindness, goodness, faithfulness, humility, and self-control, as the gifts of the Spirit (Gal. 5:22). It is through the eyes of the spirit that we can truly appreciate the value of those we are called to serve, and the value of serving others.

The Scriptures teach us that God has poured out his Spirit on every nation and every person (1 Cor. 12). Therefore, we can say, that our relationship with God, is in a sense interwoven with our day-to-day interaction with other people. Namely, the reality of our faith is expressed through our actions directed toward others.

It follows from the three dimensions of human existence, that three types of human interactions are possible: (1) physical contacts (as manifested in touching, hugging, kissing, slapping, good or bad deeds), (2) psychological contacts (manifested in interpersonal communication, and meanings that are conveyed from one person to another), and (3) spiritual contacts, whereby meanings that otherwise would have been impossible to communicate are transmitted and comprehended.

Spiritual relationships characterize our most intimate relationships. Through our spiritual relationships with others, we experience a new kind of relatedness, which includes the human and the more-than-human. Through our spiritual relationships we experience an ultimate relatedness to humanity as a whole, as well as to God. Through our relatedness, through the dimension of the spirit, we are able to receive, to communicate--and to radiate--God's infinite love.

As mentioned earlier, the essence of our humanness lies in the unity of the three dimensions of our existence. 'On the somatic dimension, our freedom is very limited. We are seldom able to exert conscious control over most physical factors. The lack of freedom at this level is often referred to as fate. Fate, in other words, is *"that regarding which we have no choice at a particular time"* Lukas, 1988; p. 164).

Many people who function from an external locus of control see their destiny as determined by fate. Some of them have been conditioned into behavior patterns that abide by laws and regulations set by others in authority.

Others seek to please others to the extent of losing their own identity. Helping these individuals realize their own inner potentials and power in order to facilitate their will to free themselves from the rigid boundaries they have, in a sense, imposed on themselves by letting others take control over their life, and to enable them to establish their own, autonomous, inner authority might be beneficial in assisting in the process of overcoming their difficulties.

In other words, "freedom from" is what many people in our highly industrialized society often long to experience (Lukas, 1986). With the realization of "freedom from," comes the recognition of what freedom really is: It is the ability to arrange one's environment; it is the ability to take a stand, and engage in voluntary behaviors. In other words, freedom is that *"regarding which we are free to decide at a particular time"* (Lukas, 1986; p. 164).

Freedom entails free-will, and responsibility (Fabry, 1994; p. 114). Responsibility is the realization that one has many possibilities to choose from, but, that, at the same time, one is responsible for his or her choices (Frankl, 1965).

Through the exercise of free-will, one forsakes the "convenient" state of "homeostasis" maintained by external law, and enters the realm of dynamic forces in need of being tamed and balanced. At this point, one is said to operate from an internal locus of control. Such a person realizes the freedom he or she has in making choices in each particular instant, and relies on his or her own value system in making decisions.

The ability to exercise our free-will, all by itself, however, is a double-edged sword. For even though we are aware of our choices, and have a myriad of rules telling us what to do--and what not to do--in case we are faced with a particular situation, we often have a very hard time deciding just which particular law applies to the situation we find ourselves in. How often when facing value conflicts we wish we had the perfect answer!

Life is an endless question-and-answer period. As to the answers, we can only answer to life by answering for our lives. Responding to life, therefore, means to be responsible for our lives (Frankl, 1965). Responsibility, in this case, goes beyond being responsible to an internal authority, it entails being response-able before someone, namely, it means being responsible to God. The freedom that we experience in the spiritual dimension is *Freedom-to* (Fabry, 1994; p. 114); the freedom to respond to the voice of our conscience, according to our best abilities. The person who is able to operate at this level of functioning can be said to operate from a *transcendent locus of control*.

When we operate from a transcendent locus of control we realize that, life can be made meaningful in a threefold way:

First, through what we give to life (in terms of creative works); second, by what we take from the world (in terms of our experiencing values); and third, through our attitudes, the stand we take toward a fate that can no longer change (e.g., an incurable disease, natural disasters, death, etc.; Fabry, 1994; pp. 81-83).

When we function from a transcendent locus of control, then, in a sense, we unravel the essence of our being. We re-discover ourselves as we come to a full appreciation of our choices and uniqueness. We recognize our ability to reach beyond ourselves, and also an inner call to do so. In response to the voice of our conscience we are able to liberate ourselves from the bondage imposed on us by the world, and we are capable of generating self-transcendent love.

The life and death of Jesus is an example of such self-transcendent love. Self-transcendent love, as He showed us, is the product of a life lived under God, a life derived from God, and a life reaching out toward God. The real ministry of Jesus can never be understood apart from his closeness to God. Jesus found freedom for his life, as he accepted personal responsibility in the search for meaning. He found meaning as he exercised his freedom, under God, in service (Leslie, 1965).

What better guidelines could we find for the resolution of our everyday conflicts than those given by our wonderful Counselor, who said: "*...love one another, as I have loved you, so you must love one another*" (John 13:34).

Meaning universals are meanings which apply in standard situations (Fabry, 1994; pp. 103-104). The ultimate meaning of our life, in our Lord's example, is to serve God and others. Universal meanings, on the other hand, imply universal values (Fabry, 1994; pp. 55-56).

Hereby, I would like to make a distinction between two kinds of universal values, universal moral values, and universal spiritual values. A universal moral value is a value guiding our relationship with other people. A universal spiritual value is a value guiding our relationship with God.

The nature and relationship between these two ultimate values is, perhaps, best illustrated with an everyday example: When we really and truly love somebody, we experience great happiness and joy. This happiness, to which I will refer to as "*true happiness*," as a result of this love is not a by-product of self-deception. True love and true happiness do not fade away with the passing of the years. On the contrary, they get stronger, deeper, more intimate, and--to use a logotherapeutic term--more spiritual. True love is not blind on the contrary it is "value discerning" (Frankl, 1985; p. 91).

The term value discerning means that only the person who truly loves someone can appreciate his or her true personality, beauty, and value (Frankl, 1975; p 37). Such love creates happiness, which reinforces the pursuit of love (Ungar, 1994). The experience of true happiness "proves" that we truly love someone, and "improves" our relationship with the beloved person.

Often, when we love someone, we experience a need to express our feelings toward that person. We want to do something for him or her and we want to help him or her in any way we can. A simple little gift, a pleasant smile, an encouraging word, a hug, or volunteering to carry out an unpleasant task--even as simple as taking up household chores--can mean so 'much in times when others rely on our encouragement.

It is through these activities that our love really comes to life. The more we do for others, the more we realize how much there is still to be done.

The more we do for one person, the more sensitive we become to the needs of others. Therefore, the more zealous we become serving the "destitute," the "needy," and the "blind." For through serving others, we are richly blessed ourselves. When we give one from ours, we receive ten in return, and when we give ten from ours, we receive a hundred in return.

When we listen to the voice of our conscience carefully, we are able to discern the voice of the transcendent. In that moment we sense our unity with God. In that moment we come to know the love of God, which surpasses all understanding, uniting us, mortals, with the immortal and ever-lasting.—Then, we wish we would never forget that happiness we experienced when we encountered God again, for the first time.

In that instant, we received a hint from heaven as to the mission of our life: All of us are called to love our God with all our heart, with all our soul, with all our mind, and with all our strength. And all of us are called to love our neighbors as we love ourselves. "*There is no other commandment greater than these two*" (Mark 12:23-28).

Love is doing for others. To a certain extent, love is self-sacrifice. Rarely is one confronted with situations that require a choice between life and death. Yet, in one way or the other, all of us are called to be messengers of God. All of us are called to lead a saintly life through the acceptance of God's invitation to serve Him through serving others. The saints of the "inner city," the saints of everyday life, are those ordinary people who treat every person as extraordinary.

None of us is freed from the limitations of human existence, and none of us is exempt from suffering. As Paul Tournier wrote, '*...there is no life which, from birth does not already have to carry the weight of hereditary weaknesses, no life which does not suffer emotional shocks in childhood, which does not suffer daily injustices, hindrances, injuries, and disappointments. To all this pain must be added sickness, material difficulties, bereavement, old age, worry about loved ones-, and accidents. In the lives of even the most privileged there--is something that is hard to accept'* (Barnes, 1993; pp. 16-17).

Like two triangles, juxtaposed, one on top of the other, there is no life which consists of light only, without a shadow. There is no life free of thorns. Yet, through the Spirit, through our relationship with God, we are called to rediscover ourselves again, and again. We are called to obtain sight of our uniqueness, choice, responsibility, and ability to respond to the voice of our conscience. We are called to rise above--to transcend--the hindrances of distress, anguish, and despair, and-to glow like comets passing in the darkness of the night--not despite of all the pain we experience, but to shine with all the pain in our life.

One of the tasks of logotherapy is to bring about reconciliation and to bring consolation. This is the point where logotherapy touches religion. The goal of psychotherapy, and therefore of logotherapy, is health. The goal of religion is essentially different: it is salvation. Yet, we recognize that although religion may not aim at mental health, it may result in it. In a similar vein, while psychotherapy may not aim at salvation, it may result in it (Frankl, 1967; pp. 45-46).

Psychotherapy and counseling do not exist for converting (Barnes, 1994). Through psychotherapy, and through counseling, we extend to others--through the Spirit--what we ourselves are (Barnes, 1994; p. 24). This in turn, helps our clients realize that all of us have been created in the image of God; that all of us are equally loved by God; and all of us are awaited by God. No matter what our physical or mental condition might be, we have an inexplicably sublime mission, which gives our life unlimited meaning and dignity.

When we grasp the purpose of our existence and find meaning in life, then what we sense--as a reality permeating our entire being and overarching all suffering--is gratitude. We are thankful upon the recognition of the greatness of our Creator, who, by granting us freedom and dignity, also allowed for our choice between stagnation and growth. Who, of His infinite power, has, yet, drawn us a step closer to himself, by showing us--through once becoming like one of us--how to bear all suffering, how to triumph over our temptations, and how to love unconditionally. Who, of His infinite grace, entrusted us with the task of being active participants in His creation and His wonderful act of hallowing the world. Indeed, in such times, we experience healing through meaning.

Often, meaning sets the pace for *Healing*. Therefore, a therapist's view of him or herself, as well as of his or her client is very important.

A logo-therapeutically grounded approach to psychotherapy asserts that we are "*much more religious, more spiritual, and more moral than we can appear even to our own eyes*" (Pacciola, 1993; p. 95), because we have been given the same ineffable gift of God: *the Spirit*. It is the Spirit through which God calls each one of us to find meaning in life even when we are confronted with a seemingly helpless situation. Through *Self-transcendence*, we are called to reach beyond ourselves and to find the meaning of life in every situation.

As therapists we should, on occasion, take time to remind our clients, as well as ourselves of who we really are. In our increasingly mechanized world, it is ever so easy to be over concerned about little unimportant details, and so easy to lose sight of ultimate truths.

It is ever so tempting to get entangled by the intricate confusion of everyday events, and to forget about our goals, and the task that awaits us. It is ever so convenient to get caught up by the glamour of the world, by what "everybody else is doing" and to lose sight of what we, in particular, are called to do. It is ever so hard to be perceptive of our environment, to recognize the small, everyday wonders of the world; to believe in miracles, and to have unrelenting faith.

Our forefathers, many thousand years ago, believed in a fierce, and revengeful God, who would punish sinners with fire and hell. --Two thousand years ago, the same merciful God sent His only Son to live and die like one of us, and to die for the sins of the world....

We should never forget that the same mighty and glorious God who created the world, stands by our side today, as we enter a new age and face new challenges.

Our Creator remains as close to us today, as He was at the beginning of time. As in the words of John 1:1-5: "*Before the world was created, the Word already existed; he was with God. From the very beginning the Word was with God. Through him God made all things; not one thing in all creation was made without him. The Word was the source of life, and this life brought light to mankind. The light shines through the darkness, and the darkness has never put it out.*" (John 1:1-5).

As counselors, we are never alone. There is someone working at our side, today, tomorrow, and always. Indeed, it just takes a little willingness on our part to take off our masks to recognize the face of God among us.

Chapter II

Seeds of Reconciliation in Logotherapy

"As we know life in ourselves, we want to understand life in the universe, in order to enter into harmony with it. Physically we are always trying to do this. But that is not the primary matter; for the great issue is that we shall achieve spiritual harmony. Just to recognize this fact is to have begun to see a part of life clearly." (Albert Einstein, 2000)

Introduction:

According to the Oxford American Dictionary (1980), reconciliation as a verb ("to reconcile") has at least three distinct meanings: (1) "to restore friendship between (people) after an estrangement or quarrel;" (2) "to induce (a person or oneself) to accept an unwelcome fact or situation;" and (3) "to bring (facts or statements) into harmony or compatibility when they appear to conflict."

Roget's Thesaurus (1961) lists the connotations of the verb "reconcile" as: "adjust, attune, accord, (harmony)"; and "propitiate, placate, conciliate (peace)."

Although the above definition of reconciliation roughly corresponds to the task of psychotherapists, and logo therapists, the word *"reconciliation"* is seldom identified as the goal of therapy in the helping professions. Yet, reconciliation is a word that is widely used in everyday language; traditionally used by humanitarians; and emphasized by theologians.

Subsequently, the question arises: "*What is the meaning of reconciliation?*" And, more specifically, "*What is the meaning of reconciliation in the helping professions?*"

This study will attempt to find an answer to the above mentioned questions through the use of a phenomenological-hermeneutic investigation. The data for this research will be collected from the presenter's own clinical practice, using the principles of Viktor E. Frankl's Logotherapy.

Method

A Phenomenological-hermeneutic Investigation:

The process of the phenomenological-hermeneutic investigation (Jackson & Patton, 1992; Ellis, 1998) is two-fold: First, the researcher has to start with a phenomenological description of her pre-assumptions of the phenomenon under investigation. --In this case, the focus of the study: reconciliation. Next, she has to gather data on this phenomenon through direct observation, and inquiry. The data has to be recorded. --In the second phase of the study, the researcher systematically analyzes the data in order to further her conceptual understanding of the phenomenon. During this hermeneutical process, she uses and inductive-deductive process, followed by a summary of the results and highlighting the new information gained. This new information can provide ground for further studies in this field.

Research Question:

This research will be limited in its scope to understanding the meaning of reconciliation in Viktor E. Frankl's Logotherapy. Thus, the research question: "*What is the meaning of reconciliation in Logotherapy?*" will be used to guide this study.

Our Assumptions about Reconciliation:

Below, we will state five assumptions that we think influence my outlook, from the very start of the research. These five assumptions will guide my inquiry into the understanding of the above stated research question:

1. In light of the dictionary definition of reconciliation, we assume that reconciliation can occur in three ways: (a) intra-personally, within a person (such as in coming to terms with one's feelings, past, or frustration); (b) inter personally (such as in reconciling with family members, friends, etc. Inter-personal reconciliation can occur at a larger scale (I.e., among nations, cultures, or segments of society). (c) At an even broader scope than the former two, reconciliation can occur between the individual, and the world; the individual, or group, and the transcendent. This form of reconciliation would be termed *Trans-personal reconciliation.*

2. We assume that one's view of the transcendent determines reconciliation with it; and one's view of the transcendent affects the view of the self.

3. Reconciliation can be a value that is intended, desired, but, as a value, might not be always achieved.

4. Reconciliation can be a vehicle of the search for meaning.

5. Reconciliation can be seen each time meaning is discovered.

Data Collection:

Data was collected from five case examples from the first author's everyday practice. All of the clients were seen on one day, which was randomly selected from his usual five-day workload. His experiences and observations in working with these clients will be recorded, and subjected to a hermeneutic investigation. All clients gave formal informed consent for the present research study. (Transcribed dialogues from sessions have been omitted to preserve the confidentiality of all participants).

Analysis of the Results:

Logotherapy was used as the main form of treatment in all of the studied cases, combined with family therapy, cognitive-behavioral elements, and relaxation training with guided imagery.

Initially, we set out to explore the relationship between meaning and reconciliation. Five assumptions about reconciliation and meaning were posited:

1. Reconciliation can occur in three ways:

Our first assumption was that reconciliation can occur (a) "*intra-personally*" within a person, as in coming to terms with one's feelings, past, or frustration; (b) "*inter-personally*" as in reconciling with family members, friends, or, at a larger scale, among nations, cultures, segments of society; (c) a third dimension is reconciliation between the individual, or group, and the Transcendent. Such quest is guided by the metaphysical question: "*What is intended?*" "*What is my purpose in life?*"

Therefore, an individual or group's attempt for "*Trans-personal reconciliation*" appears to be in the search for meaning. This assumption seemed to have been to be supported indirectly in all of the five cases: In all of the five cases, we found that clients were concerned about either disharmony that is internal (such as a case of endogenous depression and trying to come to terms with trauma), or inter-personal discord (such as family conflict, and conflicts in the relationships). The search for meaning was evident in their attempts at coping and reaching out for help.

Through four of our cases, we gained a clear picture of the source of intra-personal conflict. This lies in the dimensional ontology of vulnerability of body and mind, but intactness of the human spirit. This was evident in the case of symptoms of endogenous depression, anxiety, dealing with events that occur in one's area of fate. These vulnerabilities can distort and disrupt one's sense of meaning in life. However, in logotherapy, the resources in the dimension of the spirit are mobilized. In most of our cases, this was accomplished through De-reflection; we observed one example for the use of Paradoxical Intention, and another of Modification of Attitudes through the use of the Socratic Dialogue. Although our investigation is limited in its scope to report on the outcome of one session only, overall there seemed to be an improvement in clients' functioning, on the basis of subjective reports and feedback, such as: smiling, saying "thank you," and demonstrating a hopeful attitude.

2. One's view of the transcendent determines reconciliation with it; and one's view of the transcendent affects the view of the self:

The "Transcendent" was not directly discussed during the therapy meetings. Rather, the focus was on clients' search for deeper meaning in life. Accordingly, "reconciliation with the Transcendent" seems to have been present in the form of "seeing meaning in life" or "seeing a personal goal," or not.

The results with our participants point to the relevant preventive and curative effect of meaning-orientation, which can be fostered in logotherapy. Since meanings are not only subjective but transcendent, in the search for "*Logos*" one can recognize a search for "what is intended." – "*What is intended*," heard through connecting with the "transcendent," or "Higher Power," or "God."

3. Reconciliation can be a value that is intended, desired, but, as a value, might not be always achieved:

In one case inter-personal reconciliation was directly sought for. Another case was a good example of when inter-personal reconciliation was intended as a value but was not possible to achieve because it was not the most meaningful choice under the circumstances (This was a physically abusive relationship).

This was an atypical situation, because it appears that although inter-personal reconciliation is a value, it is not always a meaningful choice. In other words, the possibility of reconciliation as a value has to be rank-ordered with help from one's conscience. This can be done only after a realistic and careful examination of one's unique situation. Once this rank ordering is complete, there can be intra-personal reconciliation even if such is not affirmed by others.

4. Reconciliation can be a vehicle of the search for meaning:

The experience with our cases seems to support the idea that reconciliation can be intended as a value through which meanings can be found. More precisely, intra-personal conflict and inter-personal conflict can propel trans-personal reconciliation and a search for deeper meaning in life. Trans-personal conflict – a feeling of not living in good harmony with the transcendent – can also propel the search for deeper meaning in life. However, in addition to the above hypothesis, it appears that the search for deeper meaning in life can also propel trans-personal reconciliation.

5. Reconciliation can be seen each time meaning is gained:

Trans-personal reconciliation (when Noos-meets Logos) in the form of discovering purposeful goals appears inherent in meaning-seeking. (Frankl, V., 1984) Intra-personal and inter-personal reconciliation can be the consequence, but they do not always ensue as a result of finding meaning. Whether one sees meaning in intra-personal or inter-personal reconciliation depends on one's sense of purpose in life, which, on the other hand, derives its meaning from Trans-personal reconciliation.

Further Observation:

If Logotherapy can be used to foster clients' sense of meaning in life, then it can contribute also to trans-personal reconciliation, and vice versa.

Trans-personal reconciliation can be thought of in terms of spirituality, or religion.

In regard to spirituality and psychotherapy, Frankl's theory could be considered genuinely spiritual. However, in its essence, Frankl's theory is not a "spiritualist" theory. Its focus is the person as a whole--it is holistic.

Evidently trans-personal reconciliation occupies a paramount role among the three types of reconciliation: In light of one's sense of meaning in life is intra- and inter-personal reconciliation meaningful.

Given that trans-personal reconciliation is akin to the search for meaning, even though meanings are not always seen (trans-personal reconciliation might not be achieved)--life has unconditional meaning. Thus, trans-personal reconciliation as a possibility is always present.

Conclusions:

The above study employed a phenomenological-hermeneutic approach in understanding the relationship between reconciliation and finding meaning in life, as fostered by Viktor Frankl's Logotherapy.

Three types of reconciliation were identified at the beginning of the study (1) intra-personal reconciliation; (2) inter-personal reconciliation; and (3) trans-personal reconciliation. Based on a limited sample, this phenomenological-hermeneutic study seemed to confirm the existence of these separate dimensions of reconciliation.

A hermeneutic methodology indicated that, as values, all of the above can be aimed for, albeit not always achieved.

Trans-personal reconciliation seems most similar to the *"Search for Meaning,"* which can be evident in questions such as `What is intended?" What is the meaning of my life?"*

Trans-personal reconciliation appeared to have a paramount role among the three dimensions of reconciliation, in that intra- and inter-personal reconciliation seemed to acquire their concrete meaningfulness in light of one's trans-subjective sense of life's meaningfulness.

It can be extrapolated from these results that, since unconditional meaning is ever present, so is the possibility for trans-personal reconciliation.

Practical Implications:

Viktor Frankl's Logotherapy was developed directly to help to ease humanity's suffering through illustrating ways in which meaning in life can be discovered. Our study offers a preliminary support for the fact that Logotherapy is an effective vehicle through which reconciliation can be fostered.

As such, Logotherapy offers effective and practical methods and theoretical considerations that can pave the way toward interdisciplinary studies. A bridge, that offers a pathway to reconciling differences in perspective among health care providers, philosophers, theologians, educators-humanitarians-- for the purpose of a higher aim: the welfare of humanity.

Implications for Future Research:

Because of the limited sample size, as the title indicates, we have only attempted to illustrate *"seeds of reconciliation"* in Logotherapy.

Further investigation of the above concepts would be desirable through quantitative or qualitative studies, using a more heterogeneous sample (i.e. to include males and females). Further longitudinal and cross-sectional studies could be aimed at exploring the preventive and curative role of reconciliation.

Chapter III

Logotherapeutic Principles in Marriage Therapy

According to Lantz (1996; p. 20), whose work Prof. Frankl recognized as "pioneering" in logotherapy, the goal of meaning-oriented therapy with couples is to enable them to "...*notice meaning potentials in the future, to `actualize' meaning-potentials in the here and now, and to re-collect and honor meaning potentials previously actualized and deposited in the past*."

In general, one could say, then that a chief concern of logotherapy with couples is to help them become "*value-discerning*," instead of "*value-blind*" (Frankl, 1986).

Whereas much has been written on the topic of finding meaning as a person and situation specific, individual pursuit, the topic is not frequently approached from the point of view of a married couple.

Unique to the situation of married couples is that both individuals in the marriage, are, by the virtue of their commitment to each other, affected by each other's choices, character, style, opinions, values, belief system, ideas, ideals, actions, decisions, and habits.

Subsequently, the question arises: "*What is the role of the therapist in helping the couple discover meaning together?*"

There are challenging issues in marriage therapy as well, which we may not find in working with individuals. Such as: "*How can therapists respond to those situations in which one or the other person no longer feels committed to their partner?*" And, "What could be a therapeutic response to the statement '*I don't have the same feelings for my spouse as I used to...?*'"

The task of the following study is to explore those concepts of logotherapy that would help therapists positively approach such situations.

As we will see, logotherapy in exactly these cases can provide a "*safety net*" because it does not ignore personal freedom and responsibility, and it considers what is meaningful not only as "*what is good for me,*" but also "*what is good for others.*"

We will preface this presentation with two other concepts in logotherapy, which will help us discern a positive answer to the above stated questions. These are the *Psychiatric* and the *Psychological Credo*, which are familiar to Logotherapists.

According to Frankl's Psychiatric Credo (1986): "*A person can be disturbed but not destroyed.*"

--And the Psychological Credo: "*Persons are able to distance themselves from their situation and to transcend their environment in their spirit toward something or someone else.*"

Below we will take a look at how therapists can accompany their clients step by step in their search for deeper meaning in relationships.

The presentation will be based on earlier work by Lantz (1996) and Lukas (1997) and my own experiences of using logotherapeutic principles in marriage therapy. (All the cases presented below are fictitious, with relevant personal data omitted and altered to protect confidentiality).

1. The Initial Interview

Case 1: Mr. and Mrs. X. were referred to our center by a mental health therapist. This therapist saw Mrs. X. regarding symptoms of depression, and, felt that she and her husband would benefit from therapy to improve Mr. X. and Mrs. X. 's "communication problem." The meeting with the Xs started with expressing to them my appreciation for coming to therapy together and thereby demonstrating to each other that they care for each other and their relationship. I asked the couple to help me understand their situation better by drawing a family genogram.

This genogram included the names and ages of their children and members in their extended family. As we started talking about the children, it became apparent to me that both Mr. and Mrs. X. were very proud of their children, and they both were trying to take good care of them.

I asked the couple about their past medical history and their current employment. Next, I posed a question about their future goals and hopes. At this point Mrs. X. broke down in tears. She shared that one of their daughters will have to undergo a long and dangerous surgical procedure during the next month. Mr. X.'s eyes were also teary as they both expressed a lot of concern about this upcoming event. Here is where communication between them was "burdened." Mr. X. claimed that Mrs. X. kept the children too busy with other activities for them to be able to make preparations for the potentially life threatening surgery. To this Mrs. X. retorted that Mr. X's current drinking and drug use made it "impossible to talk about anything anymore." In individual conversation Mr. X. admitted that, earlier, he did not think that his drug and drinking patterns were "serious enough" to enroll into a treatment program, however, that he realized that "things have gotten out of hand" Both Mr. and Mrs. X. shared that they felt very anxious about the upcoming surgery. Their love and concern for their children was then established a building block in their relationship, for which sake we agreed that Mr. X. will simultaneously attend a provincially sponsored treatment program, (I provided the necessary referrals). We also agreed that they will continue to come together to improve their communication skills.

As seen from the above case example, the task of the initial interview is manifold. It is aimed at (1) exploring whether there is evidence of physical or psychological disorders, which should be addressed first before therapy could be effective; (2)

to provide opportunities for catharsis in single sessions to both individuals; (3) to understand the couple's social support network; (4) to explore the level of the couple's motivation and commitment to each other, and to therapy.

The above points are necessary because strong feelings prevent one from being able to utilize the resources of the human spirit.

Strong feelings have to be vented first, listened to, and understood before therapy can begin.

Psychological disturbances have to be addressed in individual therapy, and separately from marital concerns. In the same vein, substance abuse, addictions, grieving, anxiety disorders, and even personality disorders might necessitate individual work first. Referrals to general practitioners, psychiatrist, or other specialists have to be carefully considered.

Financial concerns, mediation, and child custody issues might also be resolved more effectively through referrals to appropriate experts.

In my experience, special consideration and sensitivity is needed by therapists to understand issues related to past relationships and unresolved feelings in regard to those relationships. It is important to listen to reports of currently ongoing relationships outside the marriage because these may defeat the entire purpose of therapy. However, it is also important to know when past relationships have been dealt with, and do not need to be brought up to burden the couple with additional problems. What I find a good guideline in most cases is to ascertain about one's sincere commitment to the current relationship, and to suggest individual therapy first if this commitment is lacking, or it is not certain.

During the initial interview, I often rely on drawing a genogram. I find that it is a clear and effective way of understanding a family's development, history, and "tracking their story." A genogram is also helpful because it aids in following the "*Alternate Diagnostic Process*," which, according to Dr. Lukas (1997), is very helpful in reducing hyperreflection on problems from the very start of therapy.

2. The Diagnostic Phase

Case 2: Susan and Philip are sitting somewhat distant from each other in the brightly lit office. They report that they have been married for seven years. They have a 3 year old daughter, Michelle. Michelle is a bright child, she is occasionally "demanding a lot of attention" from both of them. Susan's mother watches over her during the day, and Susan picks her up from the Grandma's house after work, around 5 o'clock in the evening. Philip does not get home until about 7'o clock. Both Philip and Susan are busy professionals. Philip is an engineer, and Susan teaches at a local high school. Susan reportedly started working two years ago, and reports that her job is very challenging. She has to do a lot of preparation for her teaching, and she feels that Philip does not understand and he is not supportive of her. Philip changed jobs recently. He works at a distant part of the city and has to travel long hours to-, and from work. The reason of their coming is that reportedly Susan feels that Philip is distant from her. They reportedly argue a lot about how to raise Michelle, finances, or just "silly little things." The arguments sometimes escalate to a "shouting match," because both of them are "head strong," and usually end in both of them feeling hurt. Reportedly, Susan feels "distant" from Philip and wonders "if our relationship is going to last. "Philip is also hurt because he feels that Susan does not understand him, and does no appreciate how hard he works for the family.

Reportedly, things used to be different "before Michelle was born." When asked what was different, Philip and Susan said that they used to go on hikes, go boating, and dancing, and that they would do a lot of traveling to different countries together. But lately, "we have barely any time for each other..."

2.a. Listening to "Key-words:"

During the diagnostic phase that therapist has to listen to key words. Every couple comes with a different history. The therapist has to take time to understand this history with an eye to what the couple saw as meaningful in their relationship up to the point of coming to therapy, and what they would see as meaningful in the future.

The above reported case is not unusual in a sense that many young couples today are wrestling with the challenge of how to allocate time between work, child rearing, taking care of everyday duties, and spending time with each other. Susan and Philip can rely on help from Susan's mother. However, it is possible that because they spend less time with Michelle, they have no yet adequately learned to respond to her needs. They have also not been able to find a healthy balance between leisure and work. Their relationship will suffer unless they manage to-find time for each other, and to nurture their relationship, as this is the basis of their ability to continue to face life's demands together.

2.b. Evaluating Resources:

As it is the case with meanings that were realized, "...*what is stored in the past can never be erased or taken away* (Frankl, 1986). Those couples who have worked well together and experienced a lot of meaning in their relationship, strength can be drawn from this past.

For those couples where, perhaps, not many things were seen as meaningful, appealing to possibilities in the future can be helpful.

In this connection, I usually ask couples to think about what significant events they have experienced together, what they would count as their most memorable accomplishments together. Oftentimes, this reminiscing can take the form of the "*Mountain Range Exercise* (based on the work of Ernzen,

1990): "*If we illustrate your relationship this far as a series of mountain-ranges, with peaks and valleys, as most relationships can be, I'd like to ask you to think about what events or things that you have done together you would put on the peaks? What accomplishments do you think that you could be proud of yourselves together?*"

2.c. Paying Attention to Attitudes:

From the above report we also hear that Susan and Philip's communication patterns could be improved. Furthermore, that they might benefit from *Modification of Attitudes* (Lukas, 1997) to take individual responsibility for the way in which they communicate, instead of blaming each other.

As to whether Susan and Philip's relationship will "last," logotherapy would have the following to say: We are free to take a stand toward our feelings. We alone determine what action we will take in response to them. Therapy can be helpful to see what options we have, and which possibility we want to choose as our most meaningful course of action.

 In relation to this point, I sometimes begin therapy session with individual dialogues with both partners, sometimes separately. In these meetings we discuss logotherapy's view of the human person, as well as how this three-dimensional view of human nature applies to relationships.

3. Preparation

This phase represents the point where the therapist shares a logotherapeutic frame of reference with the couple. Certain points can be related to their own stories, and the points are discussed in as much detail as need may be. --The therapist may solicit ideas from partners, and summarize their understanding of the topics, concepts, and relevant dynamics.

Some examples may be a discussion of Frankl's notion of love; the dynamics of meaning-seeking; the notions of freedom and fate; hyper-attention and hyper-reflection. Although these concepts are not in themselves "therapy," their understanding can be of therapeutic value to clients. Below is a brief summary of some of these notions:

3.a. Logo-Education on Love:

Parallel to the three dimensions of human existence (body, mind, and spirit), Frankl (1986) described three classical levels of love: The first level is what the Greeks called *eros*, or sexual love. Frankl distinguished two sub-levels of eros: the purely physical side of sexual relationships based on self-satisfaction without concern for one's partner, and eroticism, or sexual desire oriented toward a particular partner (commonly called `infatuation'). He stated that while erotic love goes beyond mere self-satisfaction, it is not sufficiently deep or lasting to carry true meaning.

The second level of love is *philia*, or brotherly, and family love. This is obligational love: we are obliged by social order to accept responsibility for these relationships. From a logotherapeutic perspective, this is still not the highest level of love because it is not given freely, apart from the responsibility to the one who is loved.

The third, and highest level of love is *agape* or altruistic love. Frankl claimed that this level of love is noetic, or spiritual, which, he stated, is the most powerful motive beyond the biological drives. This level of love is truly unselfish, given freely, without expectation for reward.

In reference to psycho-sexual development, Frankl stated that progress from the first to the last can be observed when we come to value a person not only for their physical appearance, or for our emotional attraction and appreciation of their personality characteristics, but because we can truly appreciate the whole person: "*In love we see in the partner another person.. .in his [or her] uniqueness*" (Frankl, 1975; p. 81), and we say not only `yes" to our partner as he or she is at the present, but see future potentials which only we can help to develop.

3.b. On Dimensions of Relationships:

In therapy with couples I find it helpful to relate Frankl's three dimensions of the human being with his notion to the above mentioned tree levels of love.

I find it helpful to think of three dimensions of relationships, similarly as Frankl postulated three dimensions of human existence. Some helpful notions that can be derived from this illustration are as follows:

1. The dimension of the body reefers of physical characteristics that function according to biological, physical rules, and laws;

2. In a relationship, the physical dimension refers to physical characteristics, which may attract partners to each other;

3. At the physical dimension we are "like" other people, and would be easily "interchangeable;"

4. The psyche refers to our mind (perception, cognition, logic, etc.);

5. Emotions mediate between the dimensions of our body and mind, that have the function of perceiving and responding directly to the environment;

6. Dimension of psyche refers to the personality makeup of a person, how a person can be "described" and characterized (including history, upbringing, social or cultural background, at the like)

7. At the dimension of the psyche, one relies on communication in understanding another person, one has to develop ways to "work together with" another person;

8. At the level of psyche, one may have a similar personality than someone else, but is less easily " replaceable;"

9. Body and mind are both vulnerable; both are what we "have" and not who we are;

10. Spirit is who we "are, "who we form ourselves to be;

11. Spirit contains resources that an individual can mobilize; spirits do not merge and cannot be divided;

12. At this dimension of the relationship one is seen as unique, and one can be truly value discerning;

13. In spiritual relationships one can share values, capable of self-sacrifice, capable of setting shared goals, capable of giving without expecting to receive.

14. In marriage, all three dimensions are relevant.

15. The relationship needs to be built up, so that physical intimacy and emotional bonding can serve, and be an effective expression of two people's love for each other.

3.c. On Freedom and Fate:

The preparation phase can be helpful for couples also to understand where there area of freedom is. --Where they are individually responsible for their response to their partner's actions and reactions.

Anything beyond one's area of freedom belongs to one's fate. In one's spirit one can take a stand toward events of fate, such as the other person's response.

However, one cannot cross from one's area of freedom into another person's area of freedom because by doing so, one would deny the other person their freedom, and thereby, the responsibility for their actions.

3.d. On Hyper-reflection and Hyper-attention:

I found the discussion of these notions appropriate in the case of anticipatory anxiety, and resultant sexual complaints. Along with presenting Frankl's above ideas, it is sometimes helpful to explain the difference between sexual intercourse and intimacy.

Sexual intercourse, which by some is most commonly associated with intimacy, is not the only way in which partners can express tender feelings for each other. On the contrary, sexual intimacy presupposes feeling understood in communication, feeling emotionally safe, and valued. Mostly, of course in logotherapy, we would add, sharing a sense of purpose, values, and goals—having a shared Meaning, which both partners accept, and which rests on the value of their personhood, and appreciation of each other as individuals—is essential for this highest form of self-giving intimacy.

4. Therapy Phase

4.a. The Socratic Dialogue, Asking for Exceptions:

In the case of Susan and Philip, the therapy phase could start with *Socratic Dialogue* (Frankl, 1886; Lukas, 1997): "*Were there times when you were able to spend more time together?;*" "*If you had more time together, how would you spend it?;*" "*What would be different if you spent more time together?*"

4.b. Therapeutic Suggestion:

Working on improving relationships by the virtue of reconnecting with another person requires time. Finding this time requires effective time management skill, prioritizing, and developing a habit of listening to each other's requests.

4.b.1. Couple-time:

I often find it helpful to present the following suggestion:

"Between now and the next time we meet, could you please try to match your schedules and come up with a time that would work for both of you during the week. This would be an hour, an hour and a half commitment on a weekly basis, when you would be able to sit down with each other on a regular basis, week after week." We call these hours couple-time, or couple-hour. The place has to be quiet, with no interruptions and no phone calls. *"This hour would be devoted to just the two of you During this hour you can bring up concerns, express appreciation, review the week's events, and as you wish."*

4.b.2. Encouragement:

Some couples are reluctant to put the suggestion into practice, partly because they say that they communicate effectively during the day, or at the end of the day, or because they have rarely had a chance to re-connect and to set up such an hour is new to them and unfamiliar. Most couples who have managed to keep this routine have said that they have benefited from it. They reported less "pent up feelings during the week," "less anxiety of not being heard and listened to," and more effective problem solving during consciously set aside times.

To ease the initial discomfort and help the couple practice communication skill s at the same time, the following exercise can be given: *"Please think of three to four things that are special to you about your partner. Do not share them in advance, but wait until your meeting. Then sit down, and take turns sharing what you had in mind Be careful to allow the other person to finish their thoughts, and responds only to what they have said."*

4.c. Correcting the Form of the Conversation:

4.c.1. Listening and Taking Turns:

Listening, and taking turns, giving clear messages, not bringing up past issues in current conversation is essential for good communication. The therapist role can be sometimes to caution clients against what is called *"burdened communication"* (Lukas, 1997). This happens when someone derails the train of thought by dwelling on issues from the past.

Another danger is if one does not communicate in response to what was being said, but operates on the basis of assumptions, trying to "read the mind" of the other person, because they "know in advance" what they are going to say. In such cases it can be helpful to reconstruct with the couple exactly their pattern of communication, for them to gain insight into not only what the arguments are about, but the pattern of when they "don't feel heard" or "understood."

An example of burdened communication and responding not to what was actually being said, but to what one thinks was said could be clearly seen in the following example:

Case 3: Sandra and Ray have been married for 35 years. They have two adult daughters who are married and do not live with them. Ray says that he is angry many times and requests "tools" to be able to deal with his anger more effectively. These tools can be discussed in individual therapy. But when I inquire about Sandra's response to Ray's anger, the couple give the following example: They own two vehicles. Ray usually drives to work in his truck, and Sandra in her car. One weekend Ray drives Sandra's car to town. The car breaks down that weekend. Sandra is about to leave for work on Monday morning when she notices that Ray is in the garage trying to fix her car. "What's wrong with the car?" asks Sandra. "Leave me alone!" responds Ray with a "tone" in his voice. Sandra walks out of the garage, hurt. She calls one of her friends and gets a ride to work. She feels hurt all day long and does not talk to Ray for the rest of the day. Ray is hurt, too. He stays in the garage and blames himself for having been angry with Sandra.

The couple reconstructed their original thought patterns the following way:

Sandra: ("Here we go again. Surely, my husband is not an honest man. He drove my car on the weekend, and did not even bother to let me know what happened.") --"What happened to the car?"

Ray: ("This time, it's not my fault. And she still keeps blaming me for it. I am really tired of her blaming me for something all the time.")--"Leave me alone!"

Sandra: ("Well, that does it! If he wants to continue this game, he will have to do it without me!) --Leaves.

Ray: ("This is just typical of my wife!) --Stays in the garage.

Another danger is saying too much, trying to communicate too much in one time with one's partner, to the extent that he or she can not follow what was being said, or is unable to keep track of everything that was possibly said, and has no chance of responding to every point. The partner who said too much, on the other hand, then is feeling not understood.

4.c.2. Giving Clear Messages:

In both of the above mentioned cases, (1) if the partners operate on the basis of assumptions; or (2) vent their feelings on each other excessively, the form of the communication needs to be changed before its content can be discussed.

Communication has to be slowed down. As difficult it may be, or counterproductive to spontaneity of the logotherapeutic dialogue to introduce some rules, the following rules are sometimes essential to emphasize:

On giving a clear message, one might use a formula to organize one's thoughts:

"I feel_____" `when you_____, " "because_____. " I'd like to ask you to_____; "Or, "Please,_____ " "Would it be possible to _____?; "Instead of "Why can't you ever _____?" "Don't you ever_____?" "Can't you just_____?, "etc.

Another helpful suggestion can be that couples learn to summarize what the other person has said, and paraphrase it, in order to make sure that they understood what was being communicated. (I.e. "So, you are saying...;" So you think that.... ").

4.d. Changing the Content of the Conversation:

4.d.1. Developing Empathy:

Developing empathy and putting oneself into another person's shoes is characteristically done in logotherapy with couples.

Both these abilities are based on self-distancing and de-reflection.

Helping partners develop empathy does not have to be done individually. In fact, it is more effective and beneficial if the therapist, through Socratic dialogue and naive questioning tries to help the partners appreciate each other's standpoint. ("*How do you think your actions have affected your partner?*" *What might have hurt his feelings the most?*" "*Why?*').

Developing empathy may include understanding the past of the other person, and their predispositions. This might help clarify misunderstandings. However, the past can be used only to the extent that it does not become an excuse for wrong actions in the present.

Dr. Lukas cautioned that in order to be able to forgive someone, one must come to terms with one's own actions, and their effect on someone else, as well as their actions, and their impact on oneself. One can forgive by recognizing that one is not the "judge" of the other person.

4.d.2. Putting Oneself Into Another Person's Shoes:

Elisabeth Lukas (1997) developed a meaning-oriented question scheme that helps couples resolve conflict situations together in a systematic way:

Step 1:

A couple describes a conflict situation, which they have gone through without solution.

The therapist asks: "What do you think was the actual element that upset your partner?" Both answer. The therapist summarizes the answers.

Therapist: "Is it right what your partner has presupposed?"

If one or both fail to agree, they can correct the presumptions.

Step 2:

Therapist: `In case a similar situation occurs again, do you see any possibility to preventing your partner from getting so upset?"

Both answer.

Therapist: "Would this change that your partner mentioned would really help you in a similar critical situation?"

If one or both fail to agree, they can describe what instead would help them, but they are not allowed to make greater demands.

Step 3:

Therapist: "Are you ready to realize the possibility which you mentioned and change your behavior independently of what your partner does?"

Both say `yes" or "no."

If only one says "yes" this can be enough to increase hope for the relationship.

Therapist: "Are you happy about the readiness of your partner to change him/herself this way? Can you accept it as genuine?"

4.e. Problem Solving

Problem solving is called for in everyday situations when two person's requests or wishes cannot be fulfilled at the same time, or in conflict, or when there is a new situation that baffles both partners. What I found helpful in such cases is brainstorming with the couple about possible course of action, laying out the consequences of each for all the parties involved, and then letting them chose the one which they think is best for them (the one that brings the most happiness and the least amount of sadness for both).

For example, Philip, in Case 2 requested from Susan to relax in the evening for an hour, thinking that she might benefit from some time off from her usual duties. He also taught that if Susan did not work so hard, she would be less irritable with him. She on the other hand, thought that taking time off for her-self would be "impossible." She admitted that her way of avoiding conflicts with Philip was to "bury myself in work." She said that she was concerned that unless she took care of those household duties "None else would do them." She considered these duties more important than to let go of, but admitted that she oftentimes felt overworked, and resentful of Philip for not helping out.

What can be the solution?

The two of them came up with the following idea: Susan will give exact instructions to Philip before taking an hour off to relax. She will tell him exactly what she would have wanted to take care of during the one hour time period. Occasionally, they will take turns. Philip liked the idea, and Susan accepted the "terms."

5. Maintenance:

Regular meetings with couples allow therapists to keep track of how the partners are doing, and if certain points need to be revisited, and newly arising challenges addressed. When the form of their communication has stabilized, one may help them in verbalizing contents that earlier might not have been shared.

For example, therapists may help partners review a week, give compliments and encourage each other. --Also, to express wishes, or hurts, if possible, in the form of concrete requests, but at any rate, in an atmosphere of care and support for each other.

This is the phase when the therapist can also rely on the couple's own strength for resolving conflicts, and intervene occasionally only to remind them of key concepts, encourage through the use of humor, and metaphors. Questions, comments, and personal interests stimulate couples' reflection about the past, present and future meanings, as do art, literature, meditation, and life review.

6. The Ending Phase:

At the end of the working stage, couples usually report that they have extended their activities to include their larger social systems, and their families.

Couples may report that they have tried to be models to other couples who they knew were struggling with similar issues, or to be of help and encouragement to relatives and friends.

They may state that their relationship has improved not so much because their circumstances have changed, but because they found ground for their trust in each other to be stronger than their doubts.

This might indicate to the therapist that the couple had found meaning in their relationship and that they are now able to carry on their journey of finding meaning, by them.

The last phase-in marriage therapy evaluates change and uses termination activities to help the couple and the therapist decide whether treatment has been useful, and if so, gradually say good-bye (Lantz, 1996).

Couples at this stage usually share their joy with the therapist, and this can be a time for celebration and mutual affirmation for all.

Challenges do not cease in the life of the married couple, or in the life of the therapist. Their journey together was successful if they recognized challenges as an invitation for opening their hearts and minds to the search for meaning in their lives.

Chapter IV

Families in the Search for Meaning

Recent Trends:

The landscape for families is rapidly changing in Canada:

"The definition of family has changed considerably over the years—raising questions of whether a family can be truly democratic, whether women should work outside of the home, and what to do if teenagers rebel" (Enright, 2013).

CBC Radio Broadcasting reports that the definition of …"the nuclear family no longer the norm" (cbc.ca, 2012/09/19). "Divorce rates are rising;" and "…four out of ten first marriages end in divorce" (cbc.ca 2010/10/04).

Alternative living arrangements are an increasing trend, with the number of single-parent, and step-families on the rise.

Divorce and separation rates are associated with unresolved family-conflict:
(www.theravive.com/services/family_counselling.htm),
intensifying the need for skilled family interventions aimed at reducing the level of friction among family members and enhance their quality of interaction.

Therapy Models for Families in Distress:

Family Therapy models which have been developed over the past decades attempted to address the needs of families, and family members, in distress:

(1)   *Structural Family Therapy* was originally developed by Salvatore Minuchin (1974). Its aim is to "join" a family system, map existing family structures that exist between subsets of the family, identify functional or dysfunctional

interactions between the members, and to intervene and interrupt covert family hierarchical structures to bring about healthy change.

According to Minuchin, a family is healthy or dysfunctional, depending on its ability to adapt to various stressors. Coalitions, boundaries, and power hierarchies between the subsystems are explored (Madanes, 1981). The therapist is an active agent in bringing about changes from rigid, or enmeshed boundaries, and improper power coalitions, to clear and semi-diffuse structures, allowing the parents some degree of authority, and autonomous (not-enmeshed)interaction between the members of the family (Seligman, 2004).

(2)   *Family Systems Therapy* was developed by Bowen (1978). It is based on eight interlocking concepts, which describe the way in which family members are inevitably emotionally connected, which connection affects them, and may predispose the family members' ways of interaction and behaviour. Bowen examined family history, multigenerational transmission, sibling position, societal emotional processes, family triangles, emotional cut off, and differentiation of self in his efforts to help family members reach optimum connectedness to each other, with sufficient, healthy differentiation.

(3)   *Systemic Therapy* was derived the above two approaches, and was developed by the Milan school of psychotherapy, as well as by Virginia Satir, Jay Haley, and Ivan Boszormenyi-Nagy. It addresses family conflicts in a more practical manner, rather than (psycho) analytically, and aims to identify stagnant, maladaptive ways of functioning, and coach the family to develop a new structure that allows all members to grow and develop themselves.

According to McDonald (1990), we could apply *holistic principles* to family systems, according to which (1) the family is an indivisible unity, and (2) organised whole, greater than the sum of its parts. It dynamically interacts with the environment, and moves through Family life cycles and life-stages in the process of its development. McDonald (1990) proposed that families move through psycho-social developmental stages (Erickson's Eight stages), the same way individuals do.

A developmental view of family development was espoused by Barnes (1994). Understanding the unique challenges facing the family at each stage (i.e., "Beginning families; Childbearing families; Families with preschool children; Families with schoolchildren; Families with teenagers; Families as launching centres, Families in the middle years; and Aging families" p.) equips therapists to help the family master each stage with more confidence.

Logotherapy and Family Therapy:

Logotherapy literature has consistently pointed to the significance of perceiving meaning by family members (Lantz, 1982; 1982b; 1985; 1987; 1995; Lantz, & Harper, 1988; Lantz, & Harper, 1988b; Lantz, & First, 1987; Lukas, 1990). Meaning-oriented family builds on structural and systemic models for exploring the origins, history, and maintaining factors of the family's presented concerns. Dysfunctional family patterns; Limited Realization of Creative and Experiential and Attitudinal Values, signs of Existential Vacuum, and the Manifestation of Family Signal Symptoms are evaluated. They are considered dysfunctional if they block or prevent the Search for Meaning of the Family as a whole.

In the Doctor and the Soul, Frankl (1986), describes three levels of love in intimate relationships: philia, eros, and agape. The three levels correspond to his concept of the human person as a whole: a three dimensional (body, mind, and spirit) entity. Following this reasoning, families as a whole are unique, and irreplaceable entities, in which three levels of connections can be observed (physical; psychological—intellectual, and emotional; and noetic—spiritual). The family interacts with the environment (social dimension) according to similar principles.

Just like in the case of individual members, the dimensions of the soma and psyche can be disturbed, subject to disturbances or "dis-ease:"

"...*Dysfunctional family interactional pattern is either a family communication problem or a family structural problem*" (Lantz, 1987; p. 24).

Healthy families rely on the *Will to Meaning* of the members to reach out to meaning ("to be there for someone"—for each other). In Franklian interventions, "...*the therapist facilitates the family search for meaning by helping its members get in touch with their noetic unconscious*" (Lantz, 1987; p. 23).

Meaning Centered Family Therapy:

Lantz (1987) proposed (1) first, to take a "*Family Meaning History*" (p. 23) in which the therapist uses questions, and shows sincere interest in eliciting the family history, especially when shared Meaning was experienced by family members (going through a family photo album, if the meaning connection is hard to express in words by members).

Next (2), the therapist may engage the family in the "*Family Shoebox Game*" (p. 24) which entails making a collage of values and meanings the family attempts to present to non-members outside, and those they want to share and present to each other.

The (3) "*Family Socratic Dialogue*" (p. 24) is used to help family members in their self-discovery, the discovery of meaning embedded in their strengths, values, hopes, and achievements.

Regarding communication patterns, Lukas's *Meaning-oriented Questions and Answers* have been documented by Maria and Edward Marshall (2012). The "*Mountain-Range Exercise*" by Ernzen (1990), has been described as a helpful tool for eliciting shared meanings that families may want to cherish and honour.

Validating the Need for Family Enrichment Programs:

In the footsteps of the above mentioned Logotherapists, the first author conducted an observational study of thirty parent-child dyadic interactions (Ungar, 1992). Subscales of the Parent-Child Dyadic Interaction Rating Scale (Eyberg, & Robinson, 1983) were used to record the data from interactions of "Abusive" parent-child dyads and "Healthy" parent-child dyads.

The first group had been identified and referred for treatment by Child Protective Agencies to the Alberta Children's Hospital's Department of Psychology. The second group was recruited from local day cares. Data was analyzed along positive, reaffirming parent behaviours (i.e., "Labeled Praise," "Physically Positive," and "Physically Negative," "Critical Statements," DPICS Manual, pp. 39-42). The second group had no previous involvement with child protection agencies.

The two groups showed no significant difference in terms of the negative parent behaviours. However, statistically significant difference was found between the two groups on the frequency of "Labelled Praise," which was consistent over the time of the observation period, and indicated that "abusive parents" tend to praise their children less frequently than parents in the general population do.

While the results of this study were preliminary, and charted a path for further research, they support the evidence for the potential benefits of Family Enrichment Programs, whereby parents and children are coached to interact in a positive, supportive, and encouraging way.

The "Family ABC" Program:

In view of continuing societal challenges to families, and joining the efforts of other logotherapists, we would like to propose a *Meaning Centered Family Enrichment Program*:

This program would be based on the preventive, and curative factor of *Searching for and Finding Meaning in families*, and on the principles of sharing one's experience in the context of mutual support and fellowship—On the principle that each person in the family is unique, irreplaceable, and valuable, and the need to communicate and affirm the value of family-life.

Families from the community would participate in this program. Ideally, it would be parents, and their children (school age and older). Extended family members would be welcome to join if they wished.

The families would be welcomed and introduced to some of the basic principles of Franklian theory about the relevance of the *Search for Meaning*, as well as other logotherapeutic concepts from literature (which we discussed in previous chapters, and reviewed in our book *Logotherapy Revisited*; Marshall, & Marshall, 2012).

They would be invited to engage in *"Frankl's Mountain Range Exercise"* (Ernzen, 1990), which would be adapted for families to discuss shared meanings and *"precious memories of time spent together,"* *"what do we hold dear in our family today,"* and *"What do we aspire to in our family in the future?"* Time for sharing and reflection would be provided.

Consequently, participants would be introduced to the *Family ABC List—Worksheet for Meaningful Family Life* [Appendix A]. This list contains several positive attributes that may describe a family and its members, and their actions and inter-actions. It was developed by the authors for guiding reflection and sharing of values that families have actualized, or may consider actualizing in the future.

The list is provided in alphabetical order for the sake of simplicity and light-heartedness. It is a tentative list, which is open to participants' observations, comments, and suggestions.

In reflecting on the virtues and values listed, couples would be invited to share personal examples. *Sharing* would make it especially valuable for participants to realize values they have actualized and to gain strength from other families' examples who have experienced trials.

The moderator would guide the group process, and would elaborate on certain points, relating them to literature from psychology, counselling theory, or spirituality.

The principle behind the Family ABC program is *De-reflection* and *Self-discovery*: Participants are invited to de-reflect from analysis of failures, wrong doings, mistakes, or dysfunction, and instead, to engage in constructive, Meaning-oriented dialogue with each other. Its emphasis is on the here-and-now family unit, and presented with the aim of increasing cohesion among its members.

The moderator would be free to outline further logotherapeutic concepts, such as the difference between the areas of "*Fate and Freedom*," the "*Meaning Triangle*," "*The Tragic Triad*," and "*Tragic Optimism*"—all derived from Franklian Logotherapy (Sjolie, 2008)--and Family Life Cycles (Barnes, 1994), and orient the discussion toward the family's present and future development.

Lantz (1987) and Lukas (1990) noted that positive examples can be transmitted by "vicarious learning" in families (just the same as negative patterns can be learned from observation).

Questions, such as: "*Which among these attributes appeals to you the most?*" and prompts, such as: "*Please take time to reflect which among these attributes and virtues you have seen in your family,*" can be used to orient the family toward positive potentials and avoid hyper-reflection on negative experiences.

For future uses, the Family ABC list could be adapted (expanded in its contents) according the needs of specific populations. For example, for use in a religious context, such as with church congregations, a source of Meaning can be derived from faith-related virtues, values, and practices, and these could be incorporated to the list.

We hope to "pilot" this program, and to receive feedback from participants about the way it reinforces positive bonding, praise, and caring in families, and counteracts cynicism, pessimism, and an ephemeral, nihilistic attitude.

Family ABC

Worksheet for Meaningful Family Life

A : acceptance, attention, affection, agape, availability, actions, attitude, abundance;

B : "best," bold, belonging, beauty, blessing, boundaries, bounty;

C : caring, compassionate, courage, consolation, confidence, consequent, contemplative, creativity;

D : devotion, dutiful, diligence, dignity, determined;

E : emotion, encouragement, endurance;

F : forgiveness, fidelity, faith, festive, father, family

G: gratitude, grace, generosity, giving;

H : helpfulness, healing, hope, humility, harmonious, humorous, happy;

I : intimacy, integrity, individual, infinity, inner-peace, inventive;

J : joy, judicious;

K : kindness, kiss, knowledge, kind-hearted;

L : love, listening, leadership;

M : mother, marriage, Meaning, meditate, melodious

N : nurturing, natural

O : outgoing, outpouring, observant;

P: passionate, patience, philia;

Q : quiet, quality;

R : responsible, refined, reliable, reflective, right, reason

S : supportive, solitude, spirit, spiritual, serious, serendipity, sophisticated, self-giving, self-transcendent, sensitive;

T : tolerance, teaching, truthful, trusting, trustworthy, temperance;

U : understanding, uncompromising, unity, uniqueness;

V : victory, valor, vitality, vocation;

W : wonder, work, worthy, welcoming, wisdom;

Y : yearning;

Z: zeal.

Chapter V

The Role of Logotherapy-Education in the Treatment of Personality Disorders

In the *"Theory and Therapy of Mental Disorders,"* Viktor Emil Frankl, MD, PhD, wrote:

"Once in their life every person with a personality disorder stands at the crossroads this decision between, on the one hand, a bare disposition, and on the other hand, his or her own disposition to a personality disorder. Prior to this decision, we should not yet describe them as personality disorders at all. That from which the personality disorder first arises (form which it can arise, but does not necessarily arise) we could call personality instability, in contrast to a personality disorder" (Frankl, 2004, p. 144).

The current DSM-5 classification of personality disorders has recognized the importance of the search for meaning within the criteria for a normal personality. In its Levels of *Personality Functioning Scale* it defines self-direction as:

"The pursuit of coherent and meaningful short-term and life goals, utilization of constructive and pro-social internal standards of behavior, ability to self-reflect productively."

For the level of functioning and self-direction, the normal standard is described along three characteristics:

1. "Sets and aspires to reasonable goals based on a realistic assessment of personal capacities;"

2. "Utilizes appropriate standards of behavior, attaining fulfilment in multiple realms;"

3. "Can reflect on, and make constructive meaning of internal experience."

Since Existential analysis is an analysis of freedom and responsibility, and Logotherapy aims to help people find meaning in exercising their responsibility as a source of health, this paper would aim to answer the question: "*What is the role of Logotherapy-Education in the treatment of Personality Disorders?*"

To answer this question, a review of Logotherapy literature would help us gain insight about how Logotherapists have included an educational component in their treatment approach to individuals suffering from Personality Disorders.

Review of Literature

Logotherapists have researched and documented their applications of Logotherapy in the case of a variety of personality disorders:

Histrionic Personality Disorder (Lukas, 1991)

Antisocial Personality Disorder (Barnes, 1994)

Borderline Personality Disorder (Rodrigues, 2004)

Narcissistic Personality Disorder (Rogina, 2004)

Dependent Personality Disorder (Rogina & Quilitch, 2006)

From these categories of Personality Disorders, DSM-5 dropped from its classification the following categories: (1) Histrionic Personality Disorder (Emotional Lability, Manipulativeness and Attention Seeking); and (2) Dependant Personality Disorder (Submissiveness, Anxiousness and Separation Insecurity), which are now to be described under a new category of "Personality Disorder Trait Specific."

Schizotypal Personality disorder is the only diagnostic category for which there does not seem to be any current documented Logotherapy-treatment examples.

To be able to define "Personality Disorder Trait Specific," the DSM-5 provides a Clinicians' Personality Trait Rating Form where there are five main trait domains (Each domain has specific trait facets). The five main trait domains are as follows:

Negative Affectivity

Detachment

Antagonism

Disinhibition

Psychoticism

Elisabeth Lukas writes that: *"The treatment of Hysteria requires an education of the whole person"* (Lukas, 1991). She also defines ten different personality structures (Lukas, 1983) to guide the therapeutic encounter:

1.   The Insecure

2.   The Arrogant

3.   The Pessimist

4.   The Flighty

5.   The Depressed

6.   The Aggressive

7.   The "Authority-Dependant"

8.   The Intellectuals

9.   The Dependent

10.   The Lethargic

These personality structures are merely descriptions of personality traits with the intention of helping to individualize treatment for each client. However, they are not diagnostic categories, and do not overlap or correspond to DSM-5 classification required for the diagnosis of Personality Disorders.

Lukas's intention is to highlight the relevance of individualized treatment, and the uniqueness of each individual.

This means, that especially in the first stages of treatment, education towards responsibility in individuals who have been diagnosed with Personality Disorders needs to be on a *one-on-one* basis, rather than in a classroom or group setting.

Education towards Freedom and Responsibility

A common thread running through all the reviewed articles on the treatment approach to Personality Disorders is the relevance of educating people suffering from Personality Disorders that they are responsible for their actions, and, therefore, in spite of their condition of having dysfunctional personality traits, they can still make free decisions.

It is generally agreed that people with Personality Disorders remain responsible for their decisions, although the patients very rarely accept their responsibility.

A second point worth noting is that we need to make a distinction between the responsibility for having developed a personality disorder, and the responsibility for the actions committed by people suffering from Personality Disorders.

The origin and causes of Personality Disorders is complex, with a mixture of hereditary, and environmental conditioning factors, such as psychological traumas, abuse, and co-morbidity with Addictions, and/or other Mental Disorders.

The freedom of will in decisions and actions has an impact on the development of the Personality Disorders, and their subsequent treatment.

The freedom of will can be a preventive, and a therapeutic factor, if it is oriented towards meaning.

In Logotherapy, there is an educational component, since in the first phase of *Existential Analysis*, the therapist helps the client to become aware of their areas of freedom, and therefore, where they are responsible.

In the second phase of *Logotherapeutic Treatment*, per se, the therapist helps the client to search and find meaning in those areas of freedom and responsibility that were highlighted during Existential Analysis.

In Personality Disorders, we are pointing out freedom of action, creative values, what the client can give to the world, in spite of the dysfunctional traits.

In regards to *creative values*, aside from the papers on the specific use of Logotherapy in Personality Disorders, Marsha Linehan combined Logotherapy principles with Cognitive Behavioral Therapy (Linehan, 1993), with abundant evidence-based studies for its effectiveness in the treatment of Borderline Personality Disorder (Fabry, DDS et al, 2007).

Regarding *experiential values*--what they receive from the world—people with PD have a generally distorted view, affected by their own thinking, and emotional instability. In Logotherapy, in addition to attempting a cognitive restructuring, the aim is to educate the client that they can use their freedom of will to appreciate meaning in their lives in spite of their suffering--which points in the direction of attitudinal values.

Discussion

The suitability of Logotherapy in the treatment of personality disorders is due to the fact that people suffering from personality disorders remain responsible for their actions, in spite of their pathological personality traits.

There is a general agreement that in people suffering from Personality Disorders remain responsible for their actions.

Existential Analysis and Logotherapy, help individuals find areas of freedom, and to exercise this freedom responsibly in the search for Meaning.

People with personality disorders have an intact access to their noetic dimension and are able to exercise their freedom.

Existential analysis is the exploration of the areas of freedom of the individual and therefore in which way they are responsible in life--"Analysis of Responsibility" Frankl, 1986, p. 25).

Education is an important component of Logotherapy. This is because it is founded on the conviction that there is a freedom of will, a will to meaning, and meaning in life in all circumstances.

There is a potential for considerable Iatrogenic Damage in the management of Personality Disorders when it is said that "...*there are no effective treatments for Personality Disorders*" and that "...*the treatments available are very costly and time consuming.*"

If a person is told that"...*all is due to hereditary conditions and environmental factors, like trauma or neglect,*" there is no much the individual can do to change those factors. The person acquires a passive attitude toward the harm done to him or her. The therapist needs to come up with a "solution" to the problem, in terms of repairing brain activity. The somatic dimension becomes over-emphasized.

Moreover, psychological or cognitive approaches cannot be successful because they cannot alter the trauma of the past, and if it all comes down to how the person perceives the trauma...

The trauma in itself is not pathogenic, if there is not an organic predisposition. –And, "fixing the brain" alone would certainly not solve the problem.

Trauma during the upbringing in itself doesn't cause a personality disorder. There is always a predisposition in the somatic dimension, in order for trauma to lead to a personality disorder.

This thinking is in line with current research on Personality Disorders: Although in the past of most people who suffer from a personality disorder there is a history of trauma in childhood, only a fraction of people who suffer trauma in childhood develop a personality disorder (Paris, 2006).

This phenomenon has to do with the interaction between the three human dimensions during the development of the person from childhood through adolescence, and into adulthood. On the one hand, there are hereditary predispositions, on which the environment exerts its influence--and on the other hand--the freedom of will in the spiritual dimension, enabling the person to make choices which would affect their personality development.

Even though it is considered that personality remains static during adulthood once the developmental stages have taken place, this is not entirely true, since personality can be altered by a major trauma, mental illness and the free will of the person.

There are choices that would more likely lead to Personality Disorders, while there are other choices, which would more likely lead to a healthy and stable personality.

It is in the dimension of the spirit where Logotherapy can play a part in helping to prevent and to manage the symptoms of Personality Disorders.

The treatment approach of Logotherapy involves a phase of education of the existence of the *Freedom of Will* and the *Will to Meaning.*

Once these principles are accepted by the client, it opens the possibility to exercise the freedom of will to change the course of the disorder.

Once the person discovers the areas of freedom, emotional dis-regulation can discourage the person to act freely, although emotions don't have to prevent the person from exercising freedom and responsibility.

There are illnesses with similar symptoms to Personality Disorders, such as:

Multiple Personality Disorder (Dissociative Disorder)

Complex-PTSD

Bi-polar Mood Disorder

These diagnoses include a spectrum of symptoms originating from the noetic, to the psychogenic, and to the somatogenic.

Bi-polar Mood Disorder can present with emotional dis-regulation which is due mainly to pathology in the brain. In this case biological treatments are the most effective, followed by psychotherapy, in the form of Logotherapy.

In Multiple Personality Disorder and Complex-PTSD, there is a strong association with psychological trauma which needs to be addressed.

More pure forms of Personality Disorders (without comorbidity) have a somatic and psychological predisposition, and in these situations there may be a stronger noetic component in the origin of the symptoms, which is more responsive to be treated with Logotherapy.

Once Logotherapy education is completed, the client can start to look for ways of attitude modification. This attitude modification consists of moving from a victim position to a helping position, through the freedom of will.

As a consequence of Logotherapy education, the person starts to become aware of their own personality, and in what way this is affecting their level of functioning.

They are able to perceive a healthy noetic tension between how they *"are"* and how they *"would like to be."* The Logotherapeutic technique of *"Act as if"* (Crumbaugh, 1988, p. 74) within Logoanalysis can be particularly useful in moving forward.

There is an association between Personality Disorders and Addictions, and there have been descriptions of *"Addictive Personality."* In this regard, the steps of Logoanalysis could be a useful method in the management of Personality Disorders.

There is a difference between Cognitive Behavioral Therapy (CBT) and Logotherapy. In CBT, responsibility in Personality Disorders is acknowledged in the form of consequences for the actions of the individual, which "should" correct the behaviour, or way of thinking.

In Logotherapy, the attitudinal change is facilitated though awakening the noetic dimension, and helping the client to use the freedom of will, to correct those aspects of personality which are interfering with their daily functioning. Logotherapy is better-rounded since it recognizes the freedom of the spirit and conscience.

CBT considers the individual driven by the forces of cognitive dissonance and by behavioral conditioning, which can also come in the form of auto-suggestion or self-delivery. It appears that in CBT there is a philosophical contradiction which ultimately prevents the person with a Personality Disorder to correct herself or himself to be different, since in auto-suggestion without freedom, the person would have to obey the same patterns of thinking and behaviour that were the cause of the dysfunction, and maintained it in the first place.

In real practice, the gap between Logotherapy and CBT, is narrowed by the practitioner's clinical experience. An experienced clinician would covertly introduce the concept of freedom of will and responsibility, followed by a search for meaning in life, to help the client to move forward in her or his life. --From this point of view, Logotherapy education "substitutes" clinical experience in understanding the human spiritual (noetic) dimension and how it can be used therapeutically by the therapist and the client suffering from Personality Disorder.

What we described in this paper is the way Logotherapy-Education *complements* clinical experience in the management of Personality Disorders.

Chapter VI

Logotherapy and Physical Health

Introduction:

Throughout the past Centuries, and continuing in our present days, there is a quest for an ever increasing understanding of the human body, its functioning, and physical pathology, which could be assessed, and evaluated with greater precision and accuracy towards a more effective treatment.--The education of doctors and nurses sensitizes them towards physical complaints and manifestations of illness, in the form of symptoms and syndromes.

Dove tailing the developments in the field of the medical sciences is research in the humanities and social sciences aimed at exploring, and describing the psychological and social aspects of human existence, especially in the areas of cognition, emotion, personality, motivation, perception, intelligence, intra-, and inter-personal dynamics.

Increasing number of psychologists, counsellors, social workers, pastors, and educators participate in a multi-disciplinary approach to treatment.

Holistic Approach to Treatment:

The work of Viktor Frankl in introducing and developing logotherapy pioneered a new perspective within all of these fields of study and practice, respectively, when, through the introduction of the notion of the *Human Spirit*, the *Search for Meaning* and *Purpose in Life* acquired relevance for understanding the functioning of the whole of the human person in the environment.

By highlighting the unity of body, mind and spirit, logotherapy reinforced the dialogue among the disciplines, and allowed for an inter-connection of different aspects of thought and practice.

Through this *holistic approach*, it became possible for Dr. Frankl to extend the scope of the initial assessment, beyond the traditional boundaries of physical symptoms, to mental processes, and spiritual aspirations, and to embrace collaboration among various disciplines.

A Case Example:

One of the earliest examples from Dr. Frankl's medical practice is described in his book *The Doctor and the Soul*, first published in 1946 (Frankl, 1986).

Viktor Frankl presents the case of a junior doctor who became aware of a suicide note written by a female patient in the surgical ward, who was scheduled to have a leg amputated because of tuberculosis of the bone. Through the metaphor of the life of an ant, which would be meaningful within the ant-community only to "run around on all six legs," he illustrated that the same cannot be true for human beings.

This is the first example in his writings where Viktor Frankl mentions the style of the *Socratic Dialogue*. He counsels the patient to go through the operation, and thus saves her from committing suicide. At the same time that he helps her to overcome the depression, she finally seeks physical treatment through surgery. --Thus, in the same instance that the doctor manages to save her life by overcoming the depression, and by helping her not to commit suicide, the patient finds the strength to save her-self through undergoing life-saving surgery.

As we can see from this example, logotherapy not only opens the dialogue between the medical sciences and the humanities, but it reinforces that bridge by continually appealing to professionals to look beyond their respective areas.

The purpose of this article was inspired by this holistic approach as it seeks to explore *"How can logotherapy help to improve the physical health of people suffering from mental disorders?"*

The significance of this paper can be appreciated in the light of research efforts on understanding the magnitude of the affliction that people who suffer from mental disorders experience.

Review of Literature on the Physical Health of People with Mental Disorders:

Several epidemiological studies draw attention to the fact that there is an increased risk of premature death among people with many forms of mental disorders (Harris, & Barraclough, 1998). For example, in schizophrenia there is a high natural mortality, which has been attributed to environmental etiology.

This means that people with schizophrenia live an unhealthy lifestyle with poor diet, increased cigarette smoking, drug-, or alcohol abuse, and that they exercise less than the average population (Brown, et al., 1999; Brown, et al., 2000; Cormack, et al., 2004).

Similar results have been reported in the case of individuals diagnosed with depression (Fergusson, et al., 2003).

In addition to the risk factors related to the lifestyle of people with mental disorder, the adverse effects of psychotropic medication also contributes to an increased risk for premature death.

Antipsychotic medication, in particular, may induce endocrine problems (for example high prolactine levels inducing galactorrhea and sexual dysfunction; Maguire, 2002); neurological problems (for example tardive dyskinesia; Ballesteros, et al., 2000; Meara, & Hobson, 2000); and cardiovascular risk factors (such as lengthening of the QTc interval; Reilly, et al., 2000; O'Brien, & Oyebode, 2003; Davidson, 2002).

Newer antipsychotics have been shown to induce increased propensity to cause weight gain, high glucose, and diabetes (Mir, & Taylor, 2001; Koro, et al., 2002; McIntyre, et al., 2003) and high cholesterol levels (Koro, et al., 2002; Lindenmayer, et al., 2003).

Lifestyle-related factors, and the adverse effects of the medication, may augment each other. This can be seen in the case where patients who smoke tobacco require higher doses of medication (Kelly, & McCredie, 2000).

Another example can be seen in the case of patients with depression who abuse alcohol, and as a result, their symptoms of depression become worse, requiring more medication.

It is known that most people with mental disorders are less likely to report their physical complaints; less likely to seek help from health professionals; less likely to attend scheduled appointments, and follow-ups with their family physician, and other health professionals (Phelan, et al., 2001).

For example, a patient with depression lacks motivation due to his or her low mood; and a patient with psychosis may be afraid to meet other people, and would tend to isolate him-, or herself, due to paranoid thinking.

In the case of neurosis, the patients' anxiety may prevent them from going outside the home, such as in the case of agoraphobia. --All these factors can make patients less likely to participate in health-promotion programmes.

On the other hand, in certain neurotic conditions, patients may complain of *Multiple Unexplained Physical Symptoms*, making it difficult to pinpoint a real physical problem; or may use medical resources inappropriately, equally leading to a neglect of their physical health.

In several countries around the world, the living conditions of people with mental disorders, as well as other adverse social factors, amalgamate with the above mentioned problems to exacerbate their poor physical health.

A final but nonetheless very relevant factor is the attitude of mental health care professionals towards this problem:

(1) Traditionally, concerns about the physical health of mentally ill people have been outside the area of expertise of most mental health care professionals;

(2) Through our own clinical experience we have noticed, that the issue of physical health can be difficult to address by mental health professionals, because it requires an honest reflection on their own attitudes towards their own physical health, and lifestyle.

Due to the recurrent and chronic nature of mental disorders, there appears to be a need to address the mental and physical health issues of people with mental disorders as equally important, to avoid perpetuating the physical decline of the patients.

Mental health professionals are proposing various ways of helping people suffering with mental disorders take care of their physical health. As part of health-promotion, they encourage patients to reduce tobacco smoking (Addington, et al., 1998; Kelly, & McCredie, 2000; Himmeihoch, 2003), and alcohol consumption; stop taking illicit drugs; increase exercise, and eat a healthier diet. They suggest complementing these measures with dedicated health-promotion programs, promoting better housing facilities and the availability of social support, and improving the medical management of the disease through a closer monitoring of the adverse effects of medications (Brown, et al., 2000; Osborn, 2001; Phelan, et al., 2001; McCredie, 2003).

However, in clinical practice, we observed that even though there is an awareness of these measures, and they are implemented, consistency and benefits for the long-run can be achieved only if patients themselves have a reason to believe that these efforts can be beneficial. Such is the case when they see them as purposeful for their recovery, in the context of perceiving their lives as meaningful.

Since logotherapy helps patients to find meaning in their lives, we believe that it can be a crucial component of a holistic treatment approach.

Review of Logotherapy Literature on the Therapist-Patient Relationship:

Our research has confirmed that through a holistic approach to the patient and to their situation, therapists can relate to them in a more meaningful way than by considering their physical or mental symptoms alone, in isolation of their spiritual strengths, and aspirations.

Doctors and nurses who practice logotherapy report that respecting and reinforcing their patients' dignity helps the patients to gain insight about their self-worth, value, and meaning in life, starting from the initial information gathering, and gaining informed consent, throughout all stages of treatment and follow-up, and an improved therapeutic milieu (Simms, 1979; Naitoh, 1984; Starck, 1985; Stefanics, 1989; Urdezo, 1990; Heines, 1997; Wintz, 1997; Westermann, & Gennari, 1999; Rodrigues, 2002; Van Pelt, 2002; Mendez, & Mendez, 2004).

The success of the quest for helping patients to build healthy attitudes towards taking care of their physical health requires that therapists reflect on their own attitude towards their physical health, and lifestyle.

Therapists themselves need to strive for a healthy-, and balanced life; to break their resistance in approaching physical health issues with patients, and to accept their own limitations in order to transmit empathy and understanding. In this respect logotherapists have highlighted the relevance of self-care for therapists (Shields, 1996; Ungar, et al., 2000; Ernzen, 2001; Schulenberg, 2003; Welter, 2003).

Discussion:

Our current study relied on an evidence-based review of literature. It illustrated how people with mental disorders have increased morbidity of suffering from various physical illnesses, and suggested ways of improving their physical health through a meaning-oriented approach offered by logotherapy.

This review appears to reinforce the interconnections between body, mind, and spirit, as postulated by Viktor Frankl. It suggests that by targeting the *Noetic Dimension* (spirit) in therapy, a healthy meaning-orientation will impact the mind, alleviating the psychological symptoms, as well as affect the body, improving the physical health of the patients.

Traditionally, the emphasis in logotherapy has been to treat mental disorders, where the resources of the human spirit had to be accessed, and where it was relevant to retain a fundamental orientation to meaning, even when the noetic dimension was temporarily blocked (Mendez, 2004).

However, throughout the review of the logotherapy literature emphasizing physical health issues, we found several examples of how calling forth the resources of the human spirit improved the general physical condition of the patients.

On the basis of this review, we conclude that there seem to be four avenues through which activating the resources of the human spirit can improve the physical health of people suffering from mental disorders:

(1) Treating somatic complaints via medical means, and with a meaning-oriented attitude, alleviates physical ailments;

(2) Treating mental disorders within a meaning-oriented framework has been shown to improve physical health;

(3) Logotherapy can alleviate the subjective symptoms of physical illness (such as chronic pain);

(4) Logotherapy can facilitate cognitive functioning and enable the patient to think about how to improve their own physical health (such as cooperating with rehabilitation, or participating in health promotion programmes).

Through perceiving human beings as a whole, we can understand that the neurophysiological mechanism by which logotherapy helps to improve the subjective appreciation of symptoms is due to its influence on the limbic system; while in the case of improving cognitions is through activating the relevant cortical areas in the brain.

Furthermore, neuro-physiological research indicates that the three human dimensions (body, mind, and spirit) have a common denominator in a fourth dimension: time (Rodriguez, & Mendez, 1997). --Time connects intuitions, sensations, and perceptions, with desires, attitudes, and volitions.

Thus, in therapy, when patients gain insight into what is afflicting them--for example, an existential vacuum, a psychological symptom, or physical pain--in that particular instant of time, all three dimensions of their being are involved, as they experience their suffering in the form of an existential-, psychological-, and physical reality.

In this light we can appreciate the curative effect of a therapeutic intervention which targets any one of the dimensions, thus involving-, and healing the other two.

Implications for Logotherapists:

When relying on the resources of the human spirit, logotherapists provide care not only for psychological wellbeing-, but also for the physical health of their patients.

This presupposes and requires a broad understanding of human nature.

As an important part of history-taking during the initial assessment phase with any patient, it is relevant to inquire about their physical health, and their attitudes towards their own health. The questions are always individualized, and may include the following inquiries: "*When was the last time you went to see your family physician? How often do you see your family physician? Have you been referred to any specialists? Have you ever been hospitalised? Have you ever been to the emergency room of a hospital? Do you take any medications? What are they for? How often do you exercise? Do you look after your weight? What is your normal diet like? Do you smoke? Do you drink alcohol? Do you take any illicit drugs?*"

By asking direct questions about physical health, the therapist can notice not only the content of the reply, but the reaction that these questions elicit from the patient.

For example, an over-concern with physical health, frequent visits to the doctors, complaining of unexplained physical symptoms, dramatizing symptoms, excessive worry about symptoms, or, on the other hand, feeling uncomfortable with the questions, getting upset with the questions, suspiciousness, denying any problems, or a passive reaction of resignation, silence, helplessness, and hopelessness, not bothering about anything, and downplaying any concerns.

This information can be used for our formulation of the problems and the strengths to determine the therapeutic intervention required, and, depending on the relevance of the present physical health issues in view of general health, may even result in a necessity to re-focus the therapeutic efforts to improve the physical heath of the patients, and to liaise with their family physician.

From the logotherapeutic guidelines to treatment, we know that some patients may hyper-reflect on their physical health. Far from resulting in a healthy lifestyle, this attitude may result in a neglect of their physical health through not seeking appropriate care, misunderstanding of health-promotion material, and deterioration in the doctor-patients relationship.

In such cases it is advisable to use de-reflection, and to re-orient patients toward their areas of strength. The intention is to explore if these patients are trying to fill an existential vacuum with the over-concern, and, if so, to try to help them to discover meaning in their lives through a change of attitude, using the techniques of *Socratic Dialogue*, or *metaphors*.

Some people with *Obsessive-Compulsive Disorder* may adhere to a strict physical health regimen with extreme precision, and although this may result in having a good quality of physical health care, it may also be deleterious if the patient focuses the entire existence towards this end.

In this case, paradoxical intention can help.

For example, if we inquire *"What would happen if the patient went to see the doctor less frequently, but still complying with current medical guidelines?* Once patients perceive that they are able to reduce the number of appointments, or the physical check-ups, without any negative impact on their physical health, they may re-direct their attention to other meaningful activities.

On the other hand, when patients have poor motivation, we need to rule out signs of *suspiciousness within a psychotic process*, and, in this case, use their intact resources of the human spirit to re-orient them toward the meaningful area of taking care of themselves.

If the poor motivation is due to apathy, lack of energy, or low mood, we can use *Self-distancing*, and the *Socratic Dialogue* to focus on meanings which can be still accomplished, and may include an encouragement of a healthy self-care, along with building a healthier lifestyle.

Poor motivation can have its origin in low energy, due to a physical condition, such as a chronic-, or terminal illness. In this case, we need to work in collaboration with the physicians to determine to what extent the physical health problem is limiting the abilities for self-care, and then offer patients a meaningful way of responding to their illness, and circumstances.

Implications for Future Research:

Researching ways of improving the physical health of people with mental disorders offers a fruitful landscape for further exploration. It seems to open a promising perspective, especially with regard to individual cases, where research has indicated that patients undergoing logotherapy for various reasons--not necessarily focusing directly on their physical health--had remarkable improvement in their condition.

One of the main contributions of logotherapy is that it can help patients to change their outlook, in particular their position towards life itself. These attitudes lie in the domain of attitudinal values, and are discerned through the dimension of the human spirit.

Physical health can be an important component for achieving creative values, and realizing experiential values. However, its relevance cannot be appreciated apart from the context of positive attitudes towards health.

Therapists are also beckoned by the obligation to have a healthy attitude towards their own health. Much of this we can see in the example of Viktor Frankl himself, who, in the face of his life experiences, looked after himself, and, for example, practiced mountain-climbing until his eightieth birthday (Frankl, 2000).

CHAPTER VII

FROM EMOTIONAL SUFFERING TO TRIUMPH

Introduction and Rationale:

...My mother is an artist. She is an artist not only because she uses colours and paints on canvas to create magnificent impressionist pictures and images of nature--of beautiful mountains, or rivers, or lakes, or the seaside--but she is an artist because she knows how to live in a way of art—a way of sort—that is, and has been inspiring to me, similarly to the way in which it is inspiring to look at the grandeur of her tall mountains, or gentle pastures, lively forests, or gorgeous garden scenes.

Today, when I have my own little children to take care of, and sometimes the going gets tough, my memories reach back to my childhood: they reach back to my mother, and she seems to suggest to me: keep going, don't give up....This is the time when I need COURAGE.

Sometimes, however, the clouds on my "canvas" gather very swiftly. There seems to be not too much light...consolation seems far away.

For such times, I developed a simple and quick method of reflection (and de-reflection) that plays out in front of my eyes: It comes from a story my mother once told me—at that time I did not know it was the most ancient story people have ever known and told—The Story of Creation (Genesis) from the Old Testament.

A Wellspring of Hope from Ancient Times:

The *Story of the Great Flood*—which almost all cultures of the world share, and have more or less similar versions of in their most ancient oral, and the first surviving written traditions (Gilgamesh): *"The flood myth motif is widespread among many cultures as seen in the Mesopotamian flood stories, the Puranas, Deucalion in Greek mythology, the Genesis flood narrative, and in the lore of the K'iche' and Maya peoples of Central America, and the Muisca people in South America"* [source: www.Wikipedia.com]:

Noah, a righteous man, listens to the voice of God and builds an ark that withstands the Great Flood which destroys every living thing and creature on the face of the earth. Noah and his family are saved, and the animals who were on the ark. To reassure Noah that such disaster will never happen again, God promises to make a Covenant with Noah and his descendants. The sign of which is a Rainbow in the sky:

"'I set my rainbow in the cloud and this rainbow shall be a token of the covenant between me and the earth.'

'And it shall come to pass when I bring a cloud over the earth, that the rainbow shall be seen in the cloud. I will look upon it, and I will remember the everlasting covenant between me and you and every living creature upon the earth'" (Golden Children's Bible, p. 31).

There is prolific children's literature, available on the shelves of libraries. Books on *"Noah"* are available to the smallest readers, in a touch a feel format, not to mention even countless baby-toy versions available from most department stores (such as Sears, and Wal-Mart in Canada) who carry children's books and toys, of various degrees of sophistication, for the baby, to the toddler, and the small child. Small replicas of the ark, with a few animals, are among the first baby toys, and soft toys little ones can hold. For the older children, there are beautiful picture books, and even a wonderful fiction book, written, for example, from the perspective of Noah's Grand-daughter (On Noah's Ark).

An animated version of the *Old Testament* story is available on DVD: *"The Old Testament, Bible Stories for Children: The Story of Noah"* (2008).

Indeed, it seems as the story of Noah story is present in our "modern" society.

The Rainbow:

The same could be said about the theme of the "rainbow," as children's books appropriate from the earliest age on (touch and feel) connect the youngest readers (babies) to the wonder of colour, and nature. More sophisticated books for emergent readers explain the phenomenon of the rainbow to inquisitive minds.

One of the most beloved art projects in daycares and kindergartens is "painting a rainbow."

Recently, I came across a fantastic gardening book for children, entitled *"Planting a Rainbow"* by Loise Ehlert (2004), a children's classic, and several books by Eric Carle (2007), a well-known author of over seventy beautifully illustrated children's books, who calls himself a *"Picture Book Writer."* I found a familiar theme running through all these books: the love of nature, animals, and a skillful use of colour. Ehlert, and Carle's books can be found in every school and public library. (I am most fascinated by one of Carle's stories entitled *"I See Music,"* available on DVD, illustrating a musical piece with intertwined, colorful drawings of abstract art).

"Seeing" the Rainbow can be done with our Inner Eyes:

"'A rainbow, said Betsy. 'It's so beautiful.' Where? I want to hold it,' said Amelia who is blind. Betsy sees a rainbow and describes it to her friend, Amelia. Amelia wants to touch the

rainbow, but Betsy tells her that no one can touch a rainbow because its just colours. But, through a surprising twist, Amelia teaches Betsy that you can touch, smell, taste, and feel colours in a way Betsy has always taken it for granted" (http://childrensbooksheal.com. p. 1).

Browsing at the library some time ago, I found a children's book, written in *Braille*, which introduces young readers to the colours of the rainbow. It likened the color red to strawberries, orange to the orange fruit, yellow, to straw, green to new vine, blue, to the sky, and white to the petal of dandelions and clouds. This book is that it was printed entirely on black paper, with tactile pages, and it had the English and Braille alphabet for reading—A proof that colours are a source of joy to blind children!

Colour Theory and Psychology:

"How do we relate to colours?" *"What is the significance of colours in our lives?"* *"What attributes do colors convey to us?"* and *"What is the meaning of colours to us?"* My research led to several recent texts on Color Theory and Psychology which I was hoping would answer my most salient question: *"What does colour theory tell us about the meaning of the colours of the Rainbow?"*

Here are two websites I found that provided ample information on the significance of colour in our culture:

http://www.digitalskratch.com/color-psychology.php

http://changingminds.org/disciplines/communication/color_effect.htm,

Reviewing the information, made me reflect on the fact that colours have been with us since ancient times, and they convey ancient meanings that have been with us since the earliest civilizations. We still cherish these meanings in our modern world, as they arose from shared experience, and from Human Universals.

...*"Here is a table of colors and many of the meanings they tend to evoke. Notice how colors can mean very different things - it is not that the colors themselves have meaning, it is that we have culturally assigned meanings to them. For example, red means warmth because of the color of fire. Likewise, it means anger because of the increased redness of the face when it flushes with blood. Purple symbolizes royalty only because the only purple dye that was available for many centuries was very expensive"* [Source: changingminds.org, p.1].

Ancient Wisdom for Modern Times:

Most children know the colours of the rainbow; they even know it since they are very little.

My two year old son can paint a rainbow with some help. And the rainbow, in his drawings is always associated with happiness, and beauty. *"It is special to paint the rainbow, because it has so many colours." "It is harder to paint the rainbow than the sun." "The sun is nice, but the rainbow makes the picture even nicer"*—the older children tell me.

When my children draw a rainbow, I know they are happy and content. They sometimes draw the sun too. But, overall, I observed that they draw the rainbow more frequently than the sun. As if the sun-drawings always mean there is happiness right there. The rainbow drawings mean that there is imminent happiness, and joy. None of the pictures are exactly the same. It is quite a feat for them to get all the colours "in order," and a thrill to teach the younger ones "how to do it right."

There is a sense of wonder about the rainbow, appearing in the sky, and then disappearing. [There is "magic" in it—Irish folklore says.]

When I think about the rainbow, I try to keep in mind the naïve faith of my children, and I also have the Bible verse in front of my eyes: ...God does not want us to perish. God makes a promise that all will be well. There will be never ever a great destruction, such as the one that took place in the times of Noah. *"What eye has not seen"* and *"ears have not heard"* – such is the love of God for the world.

The Rainbow-Exercise:

When I really need *courage*, I imagine the colours of the Rainbow: One by one, I try to analyze my emotional reaction to each colour (I need not to follow scientific accuracy here, just listen to my perception and intuition. Others may have their own emotional reaction to the same colour, which may differ from mine. And, even my reaction to the colours may be different at different times. So, I just try to be situation specific; *"here and now,"* my view, in light of some of my preliminary knowledge of what colour theory suggests, but careful that I do not let myself be pre-determined by it, or let it impose meaning on me. At this stage, the artist—me—has freedom to reflect. The only imposition is the order of the colours as they occur in real nature—at least as best as we can give back of the beauty of the rainbow in our imaginations, and on paper):

First, the colour RED: Red is one of the primary colours, along with blue and yellow. It can represent emotions, strong emotions. It has been linked to strong feelings, such as anger, pride, and such. But, red is also one of the colours we most usually use in our culture for representing love, and passion. This is what I know from my readings. So, red to me can be pain that I experience intensely, and suffering; or joy that I feel.

ORANGE: Orange is less intense than red. It can be produced from mixing red and yellow, and is a warm colour tone. So, orange to me can represent warmth, like the sun, a beautiful sunset, or the like. Orange I am sure may represent unpleasant feelings too, if one thinks about it, perhaps less intense than red, but can stand for hurt, or trouble, or feeling lost.

YELLOW: Yellow is a primary colour. Bright, or somewhat dampened down, can be pale. It can represent light, bliss, glory, or, it can represent sadness, autumnal quietness, tranquility, or acceptance.

GREEN: I have always associated green with life and growth in my mind. So, green can be a colour of new life, it can be a colour of hope.

BLUE: Blue to me is a mysterious colour. It belongs among the primary colours. It is a cold colour. So to me it can stand for sadness, or pain. But, it is a profoundly deep colour. Mysterious, and promising.

PURPLE: Purple is the colour I have hard time relating to. It is a colour obtained from mixing blue and red. So, in my mind, it could relate to beauty, and happiness, or to sadness.

VIOLET: Violet is lighter that purple. It is the color of many flowers, and somehow I feel it is lighter than purple. It is somehow more hopeful, after the darker colours. I would relate it more to hope.

Using the Rainbow to Discern Meaning:

When I find myself in a difficult, or perplexing situation, or when I feel hurt, or sad, I find it useful to think in terms of colours:

First, I ask myself: *"What is the colour I would like to choose to represent my pain, or hurt?"* It can be one colour, and it may be two or more colours, shades that merge, and even other colours, if the pain has many aspects, or other elements. The point of this step is to get a detailed picture: *"What is exactly that what is hurting me?"* Or, "What is the suffering that I experience?" "What hurts me about it the most?" "What colours would I use to represent it?"

Next, I double check: "*Is this right? Have I used sufficient colour, and have I given it enough thought?*" If not, I may have to think more about the pain to add some aspect with a colour I feel accurate. I feel that I "expressed," "painted" the colour of the pain, or written the words in that section of the rainbow where that colour is that may represent my pain.

Then, I move on the next stage: "*Where is my hope?*" Then, depending on my feelings, and choice, I use colours to paint my hope, or to write in the hope-related words, and phrases, and thoughts that help me move on.

I think: "*Where is my faith?*" And, I choose a colour where I want to locate a good representation of my faith. I may write out my thoughts in that part of the rainbow, or just think of the colour of my "faith."

Thus, having gone through the rainbow, I let myself step back, and I analyze the picture. Mostly this analysis is a review: "*So this and this is the source of pain, and this and this are source of hope and faith.*"

Finally, I ask myself: "*Which colour (or colours) do I choose to hold on to?*" and "*How do I feel about my decision?*"

Usually, by this time, I make a decision to keep my hope and faith related colours in front of my eyes, and this helps me to simply and very quickly remember them. And, even though the other colours may not "fade away," I find myself at peace, and train my attention at my chosen colours.

I may start out with actually drawing a rainbow, and writing the words of my reflections. Over the years, I became more efficient at just visualizing it.

"*The Rainbow Exercise*" is a method of conceptualizing feelings, emotions, thoughts, and processes, which require time to take a stand toward, and which require me to gain a distance from, in order to find a *"self-transcendent reaction"* to—which is my final aim.

A self-transcendent reaction is a reaction that does not follow the reaction that may immediately arise from experiencing the emotion itself, but it is a result of cognitive, and affective reflection, and then stepping back, and choosing that reaction which I think is most Meaningful (Frankl, 2012).

From Psycho-therapy to Logo-therapy:

Meaningful reactions are those that our intellect and heart let us perceive, and our conscience, like an inner compass, point to, as the right reaction—the reaction, or response that feels right because it is chosen in my area of freedom, it is reasonable, responsible, and many times oriented toward not just my own self, but for others (Barnes, 1995).

One time, I heard this simple explanation of what is self-transcendent choice: *"When a mother stays up late at night to feed her newborn baby—that is an example of a self-transcendent choice"* (Graber, 2012). --I like this example for its pertinence.

Other choices and reactions may be more complicated, or hard to reach. Then, one looks for what is in live with one's beliefs, values, and faith tradition (Fabry, 1994).

Other times, the conclusion may be "really quite hard" to reach. At times of loss, or intense suffering, one may reach to hope and faith. One may project oneself along the dimension of one's spirit, and seek connection with the Spirit of God, seek connection with the Ultimate.

At such times, Viktor Frankl's Logotherapy (Frankl, 1975), provides guidance and its philosophical foundations *"not only the healing, but the consolation"* (as Viktor Frankl, 1986, always intended). Reflecting on one's uniqueness, individuality, singularity, irreplaceability, dignity, area of freedom, responsibility, choices, and response-ability, and resources of the human spirit help me to understand myself in a fuller way.

The Role of Faith and Religion Across Cultures and Faith Traditions:

...In faith, I offer my rainbow to God. He can see everything, and knows everything. He put the rainbow in the sky. He knows all my pain, suffering, or anxieties. He can surely lead me to Love, guard my Hope, and be my strength in Faith....

The very last step in my visualizing the rainbow, and its colours that hold meaning to me, is to actualize the meaning which I perceived: To face my suffering with a courageous attitude, to stay true to my faith, to live my hope, to love myself, and others. This step is not accomplished alone, but in unity with the Creator, in dialogue, and partnership. The rainbow is an ancient sign of this partnership, there are many other ones beside. The Rainbow is the one that was recorded first in human history, and so it carries a deep meaning to all of humanity.

Concluding Remarks:

Logotherapists have used stories, symbols and metaphors, art therapy, auto-suggestion, relaxation, meditation, and guided imagery to help their clients find meaning (i.e., De Silva Prado 2003; Lukas, 1998; 1999; Graber, 1993; Graber, A. & Madsen, M. 1994; Ernzen, 1990).

The process of finding higher *Meaning* through de-reflection, self-distancing, and self-transcendence, can be an intellectual, affective, and spiritual process, which can be described with words, and visualized.

Colours, such as the colours of the *Rainbow* have inherent meaning in them, since they have been with us since the dawn of humanity. However, it is the existence of *Ultimate Meaning* which gives special *meaning* to the Rainbow.

I would especially recommend *"The Rainbow-Exercise"* to those who enjoy visual representations, and who may be experiencing suffering, which prompts them to *Search for Meaning*. It honors the uniqueness of every individual, and at the same time, draws us into the companionship of our *Global Family* searching for *Higher Purpose* and *Meaning in Life*.

REFERENCES

Chapter I: Healing Through Meaning

Good News New Testament and the Psalms. Today's English Version. Canadian Bible Society. 4th edition, 1976.

Barnes, Robert C. (1993). Finding meaning in unavoidable suffering. Journal des Viktor-Frankl-Instituts. Vol. 1(2), pp.14-21.

Barnes, Robert C. '(1994). Unpublished lecture notes. COHD 6330 (Mental Health). Hardin-Simmons University, Abilene, Texas.

Barnes, Robert, C. (1994). Logotherapy and the Human Spirit. Unpublished manuscript. Hardin-Simmons University, Abilene, Texas.

Fabry, Joseph B. (1994). The Pursuit of Meaning. Abilene, Texas: Institute of Logotherapy Press.

Frankl, Viktor E. (1965). Man's Search for Meaning. New York: Washington Square Press.

Frankl, Viktor E. (1967). Psychotherapy and Existentialism. Selected Papers on Logotherapy. New York: Washington Square Press.

Frankl, Viktor E. (1975). The Unconscious God. New York: Simon and Schuster.

Frankl, Viktor E. (1985). The Unheard Cry for Meaning. New York: Washington Square Press.

Jung, Carl C. (1964). Memories, dreams, reflections. In: Collected works of C. G. Jung. H. Read. M. Fordham, G. Adler (Eds.). New York: Pantheon Books.

Leslie, Robert C. (1965). Jesus as Counselor. Nashwille: Abingdon.

Lukas, Elisabeth(1986). Von der Trotzmacht des Geistes. Freiburg im Breisgau: Herderbucherei,.

Lukas, Eliasbeth (1986b). Meaning in Suffering. Berkeley, California: Institute of Logotherapy Press.

Lukas, Elisabeth (1988). Psychological Ministry. Unpublished manuscript.

Pacciola, Aureliano (1993). The unconscious in religiosity, spirituality and morality. Journal des Viktor-Frankl-Instituts. Vol. 1(2), pp. 89-95.

Ungar, Julia (1993). Philosophy and Religion. Unpublished Paper Submitted in Partial Fulfillment of the Requirements for. RELS 331 (Religious Studies).The University of Calgary.

Ungar, Paul (1994). Unpublished lecture notes. "Existential Psychology". Department of Educational Psychology. The University of Alberta.

Chapter II: Seeds of Reconciliation in Logotherapy

Einstein, A (2000). The Expanded Quotable Einstein, Princeton, NJ: Princeton University Press

Ellis, J. (1998). Interpretive Inquiry as a "Formal" Research Process. Teaching for Understanding, New York, NY: Garland Publishing

Frankl, V. E. (1967). Psychotherapy and Existentialism: Selected papers on Logotherapy. New York, NY: Washington Square Press.

Frankl, V. E. (1975). The Unconscious God: Psychotherapy and Theology. New York, NY: Simon & Schuster.

Frankl, V. E. (1984). The Unheard Cry for Meaning: Psychotherapy and Humanism. New York, NY: Simon and Schuster.

Frankl, V. E. (1986). The Doctor and the Soul. New York, NY: Vintage Books.

Frankl, V. E. (2004). On the Theory and Therapy of Mental Disorders: An Introduction to Logotherapy and Existential Analysis. New York, NY: Brunner-Routledge.

Hutzell, R. R., & Jerkins, M. A. (1989) Workbook to Increase Your Meaningful and Purposeful Goals (MPGs). Berkley, CA: Institute of Logotherapy Press.

Jackson, A. P., & Patton, M. J. (1991). A Hermeneutical Approach to the Study of Values in Counseling. Counseling and Values, 36, 439-496.

Lukas, E. (1986). Meaning in Suffering. Berkeley, CA: Institute of Logotherapy Press.

Oxford American Dictionary (1980). New York, NY: Oxford University Press.

Roget's Thesaurus (1961). Revised Edition by Norman Lewis. New York, NY: Putnam/Berkeley.

Chapter III: Logotherapeutic Principles in Family Therapy

Ernzen, F. (1990). Frankl's Mountain Range Exercise. The IFL, 13(2), 133-134.

Frankl, V. (1986). The Doctor and the Soul. New York, NY: Vintage Books.

Lantz, J. (1996). Stages and Treatment Activities in Family Logotherapy. The International Forum for Logotherapy, 19, 20-22.

Lukas, E. (1997). Meaning-oriented Therapy. Unpublished Workshop Notes. Workshop held at the Eleventh World Congress on Logotherapy, Dallas, Texas, July, 1997.

Chapter IV: Families in Search for Meaning

Barnes, R. C. (1994). Marriage, Family Life, and Widowhood. Unpublished Manuscript. Abilene, TX: Hardin Simmons University.

Bowen, M. (1978). Family Therapy in Clinical Practice. Northvale: Jason Aronson, Inc.

Enright, M. (2013). CBC Radio Broadcast. www.cbc.ca/rewind/sirius/2013/02/18 (Retrieved: 24/02/201013)

Ernzen, F. (1990). Frankl's Mountain Range Exercise. IFL, 13(2), 133-134.

Eyeberg, S. M., & Robinson, E. A. (1983). Dyadic Parent-Child Interaction Coding System. A Manual. Psychological Documents, 13, (Ms. No. 2582).

Frankl, V. E. (1986). The Doctor and the Soul. New York: Vintage Books.

Lantz, J. (1982). Meaning in Family Therapy. IFL, 5(1), 44-46.

Lantz, J. (1982b). Dereflection in Family Therapy with Schizophrenic Patients. IFL, 5(2)119-122.

Lantz, J. (1985). Reduction of Depression in Relatives of Schizophrenic Patients. IFL, 8(2)94-96.

Lantz, J. (1987). Franklian Family Therapy. IFL, 10(1), 22-28.

Lantz, J. (1995). Frankl's Concept of Time: Existential Psychotherapy with Couples and families. Journal of Contemporary Psychotherapy, 25(2), 135-144.

Lantz, J. & First, R. (1987). Family Treatment and the Noetic Curative Factor. IFL 10(2), 110-111.

Lantz, J., & Harper, K. (1988). Logotherapy and the Hypersomatic Family. IFL, 11(2), 107-110.

Lantz, J. & Harper, K. (1988). Family Logotherapy in Weight Reduction. IFL, 11(2), 117-121.

Lukas, E. (1990). Psychological Ministry. Unpublished Manuscript.

Madanes, C. (1981). Strategic Family Therapy. Social and Behavioural Science Series. Jossey-Bass.

Marshall, M., & Marshall, E. (2012). Logotherapy Revisited: Guide to the Fundamental Principles of Viktor E. Frankl's Logotherapy. Syracuse: Createspace www.amazon.com

McDonald, J. J. (1990). Social Work 345, Unpublished Manuscript and Study Guide. Calgary, AB: University of Calgary.

Minuchin, S. (1974). Families and Family Therapy. Harvard University Press.

Seligman, L. (2004). Diagnosis and Treatment Planning in Counselling. New York: Kluwer Academic.

Sjolie, I. I. (2008). Triads in Logotherapy. IFL, 31(2), 79-81.

Ungar, M. (1992). Abusive and Non-abusive Parent-Child Dyadic Interactions: An Observational Study. Unpublished Honours Thesis. The University of Calgary. Canada

Web: http//en.wikipedia.org/wiki/structural_family_therapy (Retrieved: 24/02/2013)

Web: www. thebowencenter.org/pages/theory (Retrieved: 24/02/2013)
Web: www. cbc.ca/news/canada/story/2012/09/19 (Retrieved: 24/02/2013)
Web: www. cbc.ca/news/Canada/story/2010/10/04 (Retrieved: 24/02/2013)
Web: www.theravive.com/services/family_counselling.htm (Retrieved: 24/02/2013)

Chapter V: The Role of Logotherapy-Education in the Treatment of Personality Disorders

American Psychiatric Association (2013) Diagnostic and Statistical Manual of Mental Disorders 5th Edition (DSM-5) Washington, DC. Web: www.dsm5.org (Retrieved: 01/02/2013)

Barnes, R. (1994, 2006) The Antisocial Personality. In: Study Guide for the course Franklian Psychology Theory and Therapy of Mental Disorders. Abilene, TX: Viktor Frankl institute of Logotherapy

Crumbaugh, J. C. (1988) Everything to Gain: A Guide to Self-fulfilment though Logoanalysis. Berkeley: Institute of Logotherapy Press

Lineham , M. M. (1993) Cognitive Behavioral Treatment of Borderline Personality Disorder, NY: Gilford Press

Lukas, E. (1983) Counselling Tactics and Personality Structure. The International Forum for Logotherapy, 6, 3-13

Lukas, E. (1991) Logotherapy in Hysteria. International Forum for Logotherapy, 14 , 6-10

Lukas, E. (2000) Logotherapy Textbook: Meaning-centered Psychotherapy consistent with the Principles outlined by Viktor E Frankl, MD. Toronto: Liberty Press

Marshall, M. & Marshall, E. (2012) Logotherapy Revisited: Review of the Tenets of Viktor E. Frankl's Logotherapy. Charleston, SC: Create Space

Fabry, D.D.S., Sheikh, A. & Selman, M. (2007) Logotherapy can Enrich CBT Practice, 30, 100-106

Frankl, V. E. (1986) The Doctor and the Soul: From Psychotherapy to Logotherapy. NY: Vintage Books

Frankl, V. E. (2004) On the Theory and Therapy of Mental Disorders. An Introduction to Logotherapy and Existential Analysis. NY: Routledge

Paris, J. (2005) Borderline Personality Disorder, Canadian Medical Association Journal, 172, 1579-1583

Rodrigues, R. (2004) Borderline Personality Disturbances and Logotherapeutic Treatment Approach. The International Forum for Logotherapy, 27, 21-27

Rogina, J. M. (2004) Treatment and Interventions for Narcissistic Personality Disorder. The International Forum for Logotherapy, 27, 28-33

Rogina, J. M. & Quilitch, H. (2006) Treating Dependent Personality Disorders with Logotherapy: A Case Study. The International Forum for Logotherapy, 29, 54-61

Chapter VI: Logotherapy and Physical Health

Abrami, L. M. (1997). Conversation with the Terminally Ill. The International Forum for Logotherapy, 20(2), 80-84.

Abrami, L. M. (2001). The Twelve Step Programme and the Search for Meaning. The International Forum for Logotherapy, 24(2), 65-67.

Addington, J., el-Guebaly, N., Campbell, W., Hodgins, D. C., & Addingdon, D. (1998). Smoking Cessation Treatment for Patients with Schizophrenia. American Journal of Psychiatry,155, 974-976.

Asenjo, B. (1999). Raison D'Etre in Recovery: Sobriety, Service, and Sense of Purpose. The International Forum for Logotherapy, 22(1), 17-21.

Ballesteros, J., Gonzalez-Pinto, A., & Bulbena, A. (2000). Tardive Dyskinesia Associated with Higher Mortality in Psychiatric Patients: Results of a Meta-analysis of Seven Independent Studies. Journal of Clinical Psychopharmacology, 20, 188-194.

Brown, S., Birtwistle, J., Roe, L., & Thompson, C. (1999). The Unhealthy Lifestyle of People with Schizophrenia. Psychological Medicine, 29, 697-701.

Brown, S., Inskip, H, & Barraclough, B. (2000). Causes of the Excess Mortality in Schizophrenia. British Journal ofPsychiatry, 177, 212-217.

Cormack, I., Martin, D., & Ferriter, M. (2004). Improving the Physical Health of Long-stay Psychiatric Inpatients. Advances in Psychiatric Treatment, 10, 107-115.

Crumbaugh, J. C. (1980). Treatment of Problem Drinkers. The International Forum for Logotherapy, 3, 17-18.

Crumbaugh, J. C. (1983). Alcoholic Recovery by Videotape. The International Forum for Logotherapy, 6(1) 47-49.

Davidson, M. (2002). Risk of Cardiovascular Disease and Sudden Death in Schizophrenia. Journal of Clinical Psychiatry, 63, (Supplement 9), 5-11.

Ernzen, F. (2001). Healing and Growing as a Logotherapist. The International Forum for Logotherapy, 24(1), 13-15.

Fergusson, D. M., Goodwin, R. D., & Horwood, L. J. (2003). Major Depression and Cigarette Smoking: Results of a 21-year Longitudinal Study. Psychological Medicine, 33, 1357-1367.

Frankl, V. E. (1986). The Doctor and the Soul. Random House, Inc. New York, NY.

Frankl, V. E. (2000). Recollections. Perseus Publishing. Cambridge, Massachusetts.

Giovinco, G., & McDougald, J. (1994). Logotherapy: A Journey Into Meaning for People with AIDS. The International Forum for Logotherapy, 17(2), 76-81.

Graca, J., & Archer, D. (1991). Assisting Caregivers of Alzheimer's Victims. The International Forum for Logotherapy, 14(1), 53-57.

Gyamerah, J., & Lantz, J. (2002). Meaning, Technology, and Smoking Cessation. The International Forum for Logotherapy, 25(2), 83-88.

Haines, P. E. (1986). Reviving the Shattered Spirit: The Missing Link in Rehabilitation. The International Forum for Logotherapy, 7(2), 112-115.

Haines, P. E. (1987). Logotherapeutic Intervention for Families in Early Chemical Dependence Recovery. The International Forum for Logotherapy, 10(2), 105-109.

Haines, P. E. (1997). Addiction Recovery: Transcending the Existential Root of Relapse. The International Forum for Logotherapy, 20(1), 37-45.

Heines, K. D. (1997). Experience with Logotherapy and Existential Analysis in a Hospital for Psychiatry, Psychotherapy, and Neurology. The International Forum for Logotherapy, 20(1), 4-10.

Henrion, R. (1983). PIL Test on Cancer Patients. The International Forum for Logotherapy, 6(1), 55-59.

Henrion, R. (1987). Making. Logotherapy a Reality in Treating Alcoholics. The International Forum for Logotherapy, 10(2), 112-117.

Henrion, R. (2002). Alcohol Use Disorders: Alcohol Dependence. The International Forum for Logotherapy, 25(1), 30-38.

Himmelhoch, S., & Daumit, G. (2003). To Whom Do Psychiatrists Offer Smoking-Cessation Counselling? American Journal of Psychiatry, 160, 2228-2230.

Holmes, R. M. (1991). Alcoholics Anonymous as Group Therapy. The International Forum for Logotherapy, 14(1), 36-41.

Hutzell, R. R. (1984). Logoanalysis for Alcoholics. The International Forum for Logotherapy, 7(1), 40-45.

Kass, J. (1996). Coping with Life-threatening Illnesses Using a Logotherapeutic Approach—Stage I: Health Care Team Interventions. The International Forum for Logotherapy, 19(1), 15-19.

Kass, J. (1996). Coping with Life-threatening Illnesses Using a Logotherapeutic Approach—Stage II: Clinical Mental Health Counselling. The International Forum for Logotherapy, 19(2), 113-118.

Kelly, C., & McCreadie, R. (2000). Cigarette Smoking and Schizophrenia. Advances in Psychiatric Treatment, 6, 327-331.

Khatami, M. (1987). Logotherapy for Chronic Pain. The International Forum for Logotherapy, 10(2), 85-91.

Khatami, M. (1995). Existential Therapy for Chronic Pain. The International Forum for Logotherapy, 18(1), 13-18.

Koro, C. E., Fedder, D. 0., L'Italien, G.J., Weiss, S. Magder, L. S., Kreyenbuhl, J., Revicki, D., & Buchanan, R. W. (2002). Assessment of Independent Effect of Olanzapine and Risperidone on Risk of Diabetes Among Patients with Schizophrenia: Population Base Nested Case Control Study. British Medical Journal, 325, 243-247.

Koro, C. E., Fedder, D. 0., L'Italien, G.J., Weiss, S. Magder, L. S., Kreyenbuhl, J., Revicki, D., & Buchanan, R. W. (2002). An Assessment of the Independent Effects of Olanzapine and Risperidone Exposure on the Risk of Hyperlipidemia in Schizophrenic Patients. Archives of General Psychiatry, 59, 1021-1026.

Lantz, J. E. (1982). Dereflection in Family Therapy with Schizophrenic Clients. The International Forum for Logotherapy, 5(2), 119-122.

Lantz, J. E. (1984). Responsibility and Meaning in Treatment of Schizophrenics. The International Forum for Logotherapy, 7(1), 26-28.

Lantz, J., & Belcher, J. (1987). Schizophrenia and the Existential Vacuum. The International Forum for Logotherapy, 10(1), 17-21.

Lantz, J. & Harper, K. V. (1988). Logotherapy and the Hypersomatic Family. The International Forum for Logotherapy, 11(2), 107-110.

Lantz, J. & Harper, K. V. (1988). Logotherapy for Weight Reduction. The International Forum for Logotherapy, 11(2), 117-121.

Lantz, J. (1998). Logotherapy with Chronic Physical Illness Clients. The International Forum for Logotherapy, 21(2), 78-84.

Lantz, J. (2003). Understanding Benefits of the Martial Arts from the Standpoint of Logotherapy. The International Forum for Logotherapy, 26(1), 1-6.

Lazar, E. (1984). Logotherapeutic Support Groups for Cardiac Patients. The International Forum for Logotherapy, 7(2), 85-88.

Levinson, J. I. (2001). Dr. Frankl's Vita. Achievement, Dedication, Humility. The International Forum for Logotherapy, 24(2), 102-111.

Lindenmayer, J. P., Czobor, P., Volavka, J., Citrome. L., Sheitman, B., McEvory, J. P., Cooper, T.V., Chakos, M. & Lieberman, J. A. (2003). Changes in Glucose and Cholesterol Levels in Patients with Schizophrenia Treated with Typical or Atypical Antipsychotics. American Journal ofPsychiatry, 160, 290-296.

Lukas, E. (1984). Meaning in Suffering. Institute of Logotherapy Press. Berkeley, California.

Maguire, G. A. (2002). Prolactine Elevation with Antipsychotic Medications: Mechanisms of Action and Clinical Consequences. Journal of Clinical Psychiatry, 63, (Supplement 4), 56-62.

McCreadie, R. G. (2003). Diet, Smoking, and Cardiovascular Risk in People with Schizophrenia. British Journal ofPsychiatry, 183, 534-539.

McIntyre, R. S., Trakas, K., Lin, D., Balshaw, R., Hwang, P., Robinson, K., & Eggleston, A. (2003). Risk of Weight Gain Associated with Antipsychotic Treatment: Results from the Canadian National Outcomes Measurement Study in Schizophrenia. Canadian Journal ofPsychiatry, 48(10), 689-694.

Meara, J. & Hobson, P. (2000). Review: Tardive Dyskinesia is a Risk Factor for Mortality in Psychiatric Patients. Evidence Based Mental Health, 3, 123.

Mendez, E., & Mendez, M. (2004). Meaningful Framework for Gaining Informed Consent to Evaluation/Treatment. The International Forum for Logotherapy. In Press.

Mendez, M. (2004). A Life with Meaning. Guide to the Fundamental Principles of Viktor E. Frankl's Logotheapy. Trafford Publishing, Ltd., Victoria, British Columbia.

Mir, S., & Taylor, D. (2001). Atypical Antipsychotics and Hyperglycaemia. The International Clinical Psychopharmacology, 16, 63-74.

Naitoh, P. (1983). Takashima's Noo-Psychosomatic Medicine. The International Forum, for Logotherapy, 6(1), 50-54.

Noblejas de la Flor, M. A. (1997). Meaning Levels of Drug-Abuse Therapy: An Empirical Study. The International Forum for Logotherapy, 20(1), 46-52.

O'Brien, P., Y Oyebode, F. (2003). Psychotropic Medication and the Heart. Advances in Psychiatric Treatment, 9, 414-423.

Olive, K. W. (1990). Meaning in Drug Treatment. The International Forum for Logotherapy, 13(2), 131-132.

Osborn, D. P. J. (2001). The Poor Physical Health of People with Mental Illness. Western Journal ofMedicine, 175, 329-332.

Ososkie, J. M. & Schultz, J. C. (2003). Disability Acceptance Theories and Logotherapy. The International Forum for Logotherapy, 26(1), 21-26.

Phelan, M., Stradins, L. & Morrison, S. (2001). Physical Health of People with Severe Mental Illness. British Medical Journal, 322, 443-444.

Punzi, 1. (1993). AIDS-A Challenge to Logotherapy. Journal des Viktor Frankl Instituts, 1(2), 7-13..

Rahman, T. (2001):; Mental Health and Purpose in Life of Drug Addicts in Bangladesh. The International Forum for Logotherapy, 24(2), 83-87.

Reilly, J. G., Ayis, S. A., Ferrier, I. N., Jones, S. J., & Thomas, S. H. L. (2000). QTcinterval Abnormalities and Psychotropic Drug Therapy in Psychiatric Patients. The Lancet, 355, 1048-1052.

Rodrigues, R. (2002). The Practice of Psychiatry Including Logotherapy. In: The Power of the Human Spirit. R. Henrion, & C. Stefanics (Eds.). The Joseph Publishing Co., Kettering, Ohio.

Rodriguez, M., & Mendez, E. (1998). Quantal Processing of Visual Information in the Brain. Neuroscience, 84(3), 641-4.

Schulenberg, S. E., Elliott, T. L., & Kaster, J. T. (2003). Logotherapy and Mental Health Professionals: Transcending Histories of Personal Trauma. The International Forum for Logotherapy, 26(2), 102-109.

Shields, R. (1996). Meaning Potentials of Burnout in the Helping Professions. The International Forum for Logotherapy, 19(1), 41-44.

Simms, G. R. (1979). Logotherapy in Medical Practice. The International Forum for Logotherapy, 2(2), 12-14.

Sjolie, I. (2001). A Homeopath Looks at Somatic Manifestation of Noogenic Neurosis. The International Forum for Logotherapy, 24(1), 10-12.

Sjolie, I. (2002). A Logotherapist's View of Somatization Disorder and a Protocol. The International Forum for Logotherapy, 25(1), 24-29.

Starck, P. L. (1981). Rehabilitative Nursing and Logotherapy. The International Forum for Logotherapy, 4(2), 101-109.

Starck, P. L. (1985). Logotherapy: A Critical Component of Modern Nursing. The International Forum for Logotherapy, 8(1), 41-43.

Stavros, M. (1991). Logotherapy and the Disabled. The International Forum for Logotherapy, 14(1), 26-31.

Stefanics, C. (1989). Logotherapy and Nursing Practice. The International Forum for Logotherapy, 12(2), 97-100.

Stefanics, C. (1996). Experiences with Logotherapy: Nursing the Elderly. The International Forum for Logotherapy, 19(1), 34-38.

Ungar, J., Hodgins, D. C., & Ungar, M. (1998). Purposeful Goals and Alcoholic Recovery. The International Forum for Logotherapy, 21(2), 72-77.

Ungar, M., McKey, L., Guest., M., & Bernard, C. (2000). Logotherapeutic Guidelines for Therapsists' Self-Care. The International Forum for Logotherapy, 23(2), 89-94.

Urdezo, L. G. P. (1990). A Logotherapeutic Doctor-Patient Relationship. The International Forum for Logotherapy, 13(2), 112-114.

Van Pelt, I. (1994). The Meaning of Chronic Headache-The Role of the Human Spirit in Conflict Resolution. The International Forum for Logotherapy, 17(2), 70-75.

Van Pelt, I. (2001). Application of Logotherapy to Headache. The International Forum for Logotherapy, 24(2), 94-101.

Waisberg, J. L., & Starr, M. W. (1999). Psychometric Properties of the PIL Test with a Sample of Substance Abusers. The International Forum for Logotherapy, 22(1), 2226.

Walters, G. (1993). The Lifestyle Approach to Substance Abuse. The International Forum for Logotherapy, 16(1), 13-19.

Welter, P. (2003). Logotherapy and Quiet Epiphanies. The International Forum for Logotherapy, 26(1), 65-73.

Westermann, A. G., & Gennari, H. (1999). Logotherapy in Today's Managed Care Climate. The International Forum for Logotherapy, 22(1), 27-29.

Wintz, C. (1997). Nurse Structuring of a Logotherapeuitc Milieu for Schizophrenic Inpatients. The International Forum for Logotherapy, 20(1), 11-19.

Young, M., & Rice, G. I. (1999). Adaptive Model of the Addictive Process. The International Forum for Logotherapy, 22(1), 8-16.

Chapter VII: From Emotional Suffering to Triumph

Barnes, R. C. (1995). Logotherapy' Consideration of the Dignity and Uniqueness of The Human Person. Abilene: Viktor Frankl Institute of Logotherapy.

Carle, E. (2007). The Very Hungry Caterpillar, and other stories. Burbank, California: DisneyDVD.com

De Silva Prado, M. (2003). Painting a Dialogue. Presentation at the Fourteenth World Congress on Logotherapy, Dallas, TX.

Ernzen, F. (1990). Frankl's Mountain Range Exercise. The IFL, 13(2), 133-134.

Ehlert. L. (2004). Planting a Rainbow. New York: Scholastic.

Fabry, J. (1994). The Pursuit of Meaning. Abilene, TX: Institute of Logotherapy Press.

Frankl, V.E. (1975). The Unconscious God. New York: Simon and Schuster.

Frankl, V. E. (1986). The Doctor and the Soul. New York: Random House.

Graber, A. V. & Madsen, M. (1994). Images of Transformation. Audio Tapes. Seattle, WA: Second Glance Production.

Graber, A. (2012). Personal Communication.

Graber-Westerman, A. (1993). The Logoanchor Technique. The IFL, 16(1), 26-30.

Lukas, E. (1998). Spirituelle Psychologie. Muenchen, Germany: Kosel Verlag.

Lukas, E. (1999). In Der Trauer Lebt Die Liebe Weiter. Muenchen, Germany: Kosel Verlag.

Morris, N. (2012). Reaching for Rainbows. Charleston, SC: Createspace.

The Golden Children's Bible (1993). New York: Golden Books Publishing Co.

Web: http://changingminds.org/disciplines/communication/color_effect.htm (Retrieved: 21/02/2013)

Web: http://www.digitalskratch.com/color-psychology.php (Retrieved: 21/02/2013)

Web: http://childrensbooksheal.com2012/07/02reachingforrainbows-a-utales-ebook by Patricia Tilton (Retrieved: 21/02/2013)

www.ingramcontent.com/pod-product-compliance
Lightning Source LLC
Chambersburg PA
CBHW070538290526
45790CB00002B/554